HEROES

TRUE STORIES OF BRAVERY, SELFLESSNESS, AND OUTSTANDING ACHIEVEMENTS

Publications International, Ltd.

Photography: Library of Congress, Shutterstock.com, Wikimedia Commons and whitehouse.gov.

Louis Weber, CEO
Publications International, Ltd.
8140 Lehigh Avenue
Morton Grove, IL 60053

ISBN: 978-1-64030-362-1

Manufactured in China.

8 7 6 5 4 3 2 1

Table of Contents

Introduction

The word "hero" has many meanings. A hero can be someone who risks her life to save others. A hero can be the person who donates his time and energy to helping those in need by starting a charity or organization. Sometimes heroes are those who stand up to hatred or intolerance. Sometimes they stand in the way of gunfire or grenades. Most important, though, a hero is someone we can all look up to.

In this book, we share the stories of real-life heroes. Some names may be familiar—like Captain Chesley Sullenberger, whose heroic actions in landing a malfunctioning airplane were documented in the movie *Sully*. Or Malala Yousafzai, an activist from Pakistan who was named one of *Time*'s 100 Most Influential People in 2013 and became the youngest Nobel Laureate in 2014. Some heroes have won awards like the Medal of Honor or the Medal of Valor. To some heroes, their greatest reward is knowing that they saved someone's life.

Some stories come at a great cost, like the stories of Peter Ganci, Welles Crowther, and Rick Rescorla, who all lost their lives on

▲ *The Medal of Honor*

September 11, 2001. However, had it not been for these men's rescue efforts, many more people could have died that day.

Many of the heroes documented in this book are part of the United States military and have served in Iraq and Afghanistan. Some are police officers, firefighters, or ship captains. Some heroes, however, are ordinary people who stepped up in a time of danger. Lassana Bathily was an undocumented immigrant working as a grocery clerk in Paris when he helped local police deescalate a hostage situation. Micah Fletcher was just another passenger on a train in Oregon when he stood up to a violent man shouting hateful slurs at a young Muslim woman.

Some heroes are not even people at all—teams of rescue dogs were brought to Ground Zero after September 11 to search for victims under the rubble. These dogs not only had the important task of finding survivors, but they ended up serving as comfort dogs to the teams of rescue workers.

Heroes are all around us, and this book hopes to make their powerful stories known.

► *The Medal of Valor*

Sergeant First Class Paul Ray Smith
MEDAL OF HONOR RECIPIENT 2005

Paul Ray Smith was born in El Paso, Texas, in 1969 and spent most of his childhood in Tampa, Florida. Shortly after graduating from Tampa Bay Vocational Tech High School in 1989, Smith joined the U.S. Army. He served during the Persian Gulf War, Operation Joint Endeavor, and Operation Joint Guardian. In 1999 he deployed to Kosovo, and he received a promotion to Sergeant First Class in 2002.

During the 2003 invasion of Iraq, Smith's 100-man force was assigned to block a highway between Baghdad and Saddam International Airport. During a battle, they captured several Iraqi fighters and put together an impromptu enemy prisoner of war holding area. Men guarding the enclosure's metal gate soon noticed 50–100 Iraqi fighters nearby, who proceeded to attack.

The Iraqi fighters had taken position in a tower, and under intense crossfire from above, Smith took command of a M113 Armored Personnel Carrier and manned its machine gun. A separate team then

attacked the tower from behind, killing the fighters. After the battle, Smith's comrades found him with 13 bullet holes in his vest and one fatal shot through his brain.

Smith's ashes were scattered in the Gulf of Mexico, one of his favorite places to fish. He has a memorial marker in Arlington Cemetery and another one outside his high school.

On April 4, 2005, Smith was posthumously awarded the Medal of Honor by President George W. Bush. Smith's eleven-year-old son accepted the medal on behalf of his father.

▲ *Sgt. 1st Class Paul Smith's posthumous Medal of Honor*

◄ *Paul Smith's widow visiting his headstone at Arlington National Cemetery*

Corporal Jason L. Dunham
MEDAL OF HONOR RECIPIENT 2007

Jason Dunham was born and raised in Scio, New York. He joined the Marine Corps in 2000, and by early 2004 he was serving in Iraq as a squad leader.

On April 14, 2004, Dunham's platoon was dispatched on patrol to investigate an attack on a battalion commander. The squad was searching cars for weapons when the driver of a car exited his vehicle and attacked the Marines in an attempt to flee. The individual dropped a hand grenade, and Dunham, spotting the potential danger, threw himself on top of it in order to save the rest of his men. The enemy was shot dead while trying to escape. Dunham was evacuated to National Naval Medical Center and was treated for severe injuries. However, he was diagnosed with brain damage while in a coma, and he was taken off life support on April 22, 2004.

On January 11, 2007, President George W. Bush presented the Medal of Honor to Dunham posthumously. Dunham's family accepted the medal. Additionally, in 2007 the Navy reported that a new missile destroyer would be named USS *Jason Dunham* in his honor. The ship was launched in 2009.

◄ *(Top left) President George W. Bush presents Jason Dunham's Medal of Honor to the Dunham family.*

◄ *(Bottom left) The USS* Jason Dunham

Lieutenant Michael P. Murphy

MEDAL OF HONOR RECIPIENT 2007

Michael Murphy was born and raised in Suffolk County, New York, where his friends gave him the nickname "The Protector." He was known to stand up to middle school bullies and, in one instance, even to attackers targeting a homeless man. Murphy graduated from Pennsylvania State University in 1998 and, despite being accepted to several law schools, decided instead to attend SEAL mentoring sessions. He graduated from Basic Underwater Demolition/SEAL training in November 2001, and subsequently deployed to Jordan, Qatar, and Djibouti.

► *U.S. Navy photo of Michael Murphy*

▼ *Murphy (far right) and fellow Navy SEALs*

In 2005, Murphy deployed to Afghanistan in support of Operation Enduring Freedom. Murphy was the Commander of a four-man reconnaissance team on a mission to capture or kill a Taliban leader. The team was dropped in a remote area in Kunar Province. They were quickly discovered by local goat herders, and either the herders or other locals alerted Taliban forces to the group's presence. The Taliban forces surrounded and attacked the group, and they then shot down the reinforcement helicopter, killing all 16 personnel aboard.

Michael Murphy was killed while exposing himself to gunfire in an attempt to get a clear signal to contact headquarters and request support. He was shot multiple times, but he continued fighting until he died from the wounds. Only one member of his team survived the attack. All three of Murphy's men were awarded the Navy Cross.

On October 22, 2007, President George W. Bush presented the Medal of Honor to Murphy's parents on behalf of their son. Murphy received 11 different military decorations during his career, including the Purple Heart, Joint Service Commendation Medal, and Navy Commendation Medal. Numerous memorials have been named for Michael Murphy, including a park, a post office, and a high school campus.

◀ *Murphy in Afghanistan*

▼ *(Bottom left) Murphy's parents accept their son's Medal of Honor from President Bush.*

▼ *(Bottom right) The dedication ceremony of the Lt. Michael Murphy Combat Training Pool at the Naval Station Newport, Rhode Island*

Petty Officer Second Class (SEAL)
Michael A. Monsoor

MEDAL OF HONOR RECIPIENT 2008

Michael Anthony Monsoor was born in Long Beach, California, in 1981. His father served as a Marine in the U.S. military, and Michael enlisted in the Navy in March 2001. In 2005, Monsoor was assigned to Delta Platoon, SEAL Team 3.

SEAL Team 3 was sent to Ramadi, Iraq, in April 2006 during Operation Kentucky Jumper. During this time, Monsoor's team was frequently involved in engagements with fighters, and the team reportedly killed 84 insurgents in the first five months.

Monsoor was awarded a Silver Star for running through heavy gunfire to rescue an injured comrade during an engagement in May 2006.

On September 29, 2006, while taking position on a rooftop with three SEAL snipers and three Iraqi Army soldiers, Monsoor was hit with a grenade thrown by an insurgent on the street below. Monsoor yelled "Grenade!" and threw himself onto it. His body absorbed most of the blast, and the SEALs next to him were injured but ultimately survived the explosion. Monsoor, who was severely wounded, was evacuated immediately and died 30 minutes later.

On April 8, 2008, Sally and George Monsoor accepted the Medal of Honor on their son's behalf. President George W. Bush presented the award. In 2011, the United States Department of Veterans Affairs named a street at Miramar National Cemetery after Monsoor. His legacy also lives on in the USS *Michael Monsoor*, the Mountain Warfare Training Camp Michael Monsoor, and the Michael Monsoor Memorial Stadium at Garden Grove High School, which Michael attended.

◄ *Monsoor (lower right corner) and fellow SEAL candidates lay in the surf as frigid water rolls over them, a common weed-out method during training.*

▲ *Monsoor's Medal of Honor pictured with his Navy Special Warfare (SEAL) Trident*

► *(Top right) Monsoor on patrol in Iraq, 2006*

► *(Bottom right) George and Sally Monsoor accept their son's Medal of Honor.*

Private First Class Ross A. McGinnis

MEDAL OF HONOR RECIPIENT 2008

Ross Andrew McGinnis grew up in Knox, Pennsylvania. He aspired to be a soldier since kindergarten, and he joined the Army through the Delayed Entry Program on his 17th birthday in 2004.

In August 2006, McGinnis deployed to Baghdad where he served in operations against insurgents in Adhamiyah. On December 4, while on patrol in Adhamiyah with his platoon, a grenade was thrown into his vehicle. McGinnis shouted warnings to the other men, but they could not see where the device had landed. McGinnis then threw himself on the grenade, absorbing the blast. He was instantly killed. The others suffered minor injuries.

On June 2, 2008, President George W. Bush presented McGinnis's family with the Medal of Honor on behalf of Ross.

◀ *Private First Class Ross Andrew McGinnis at his graduation from the Infantry School, Fort Benning, Georgia*

▼   *(Bottom Left) On Veterans Day 2009, President Barack Obama leaves a presidential coin on the gravesite of Ross McGinnis in Arlington Cemetery.*

▼   *(Bottom Right) Tom McGinnis, father of Ross McGinnis, displays his son's Medal of Honor.*

Sergeant First Class Jared C. Monti

MEDAL OF HONOR RECIPIENT 2009

"Monti saw danger before him and he went out to meet it."

—President Barack Obama

◄ *(Far left) Jared Monti in Afghanistan*

◄ *President Barack Obama posthumously awards Jared C. Monti the Medal of Honor.*

Jared Monti was born in Abington, Massachusetts, in 1975, and he was known for his adventurous spirit. He enlisted in the Army in March 1993 and deployed to Afghanistan in February 2006 as part of Task Force Spartan.

Monti was leading an intelligence mission in Nuristan Province, Afghanistan, when his patrol was attacked by at least 60 insurgents. Monti called for air support, but one soldier was killed and a second wounded by enemy fire before the support arrived. Monti made three attempts to reach the wounded soldier and bring him to safety, but on his third attempt he was struck and killed by a grenade. The aid finally arrived, killing 22 attackers and causing the rest to retreat.

On September 17, 2009, President Barack Obama presented Monti's family with a Medal of Honor on Jared's behalf.

In January 2009, the Massachusetts Senate passed a motion to rename a state-owned bridge the Jared C. Monti Bridge. Monti has also inspired a popular country song.

Staff Sergeant Salvatore Giunta

MEDAL OF HONOR RECIPIENT 2010

Salvatore Giunta, a native of Clinton, Iowa, decided to join the Army in November 2003. Giunta was deployed twice to Afghanistan, once in 2005 and once in 2007, and he was promoted to staff sergeant in August 2009. His actions in 2007 earned him the honor of being the first living person since the Vietnam War to receive the Medal of Honor.

▼ *President Barack Obama presents Salvatore Giunta with the Medal of Honor.*

"When you meet Sal and you meet his family, you are just absolutely convinced that this is what America is all about. And it just makes you proud."

—President Barack Obama

▲ *Giunta and Soldiers from the 1st Squad, 1st Platoon, Battle Company, 2nd Battalion, 503rd Infantry Regiment before Giunta's induction ceremony into the Hall of Heroes at the Pentagon, Nov. 17, 2010*

▲ *Giunta in April 2010*

On the night of October 25, 2007, Giunta was stationed near the Afghanistan-Pakistan border, nicknamed the Valley of Death. Giunta and seven other troops were on their way to Combat Outpost Vimoto after finishing a day-long watch of two other platoons in the nearby valley. Within minutes of leaving their position, the soldiers were ambushed with AK-47 rifles, rocket-propelled grenades, and machine guns. Two soldiers were struck by multiple rounds, and Giunta was unable to advance because grenades were exploding all around him. After watching squad leader Erick Gallardo take a bullet to his head, Giunta helped him find cover among the walls of fire.

Giunta realized that the Taliban were performing an L-shaped ambush from the west and north, and he recalled from basic training that the only way to survive such an attack was to advance on the enemy. Giunta and the others threw grenades toward the Taliban and advanced, killing a high-value target in the process. Giunta then went on to attend to wounded soldiers.

On September 10, 2010, President Barack Obama awarded Giunta with the Medal of Honor. Giunta's surviving squad members all attended the ceremony.

Guinta left the Army in June 2011.

"I'm not at peace with that at all... and coming and talking about it and people wanting to shake my hand because of it, it hurts me, because it's not what I want. And to be with so many people doing so much stuff and then to be singled out—and put forward. I mean, everyone did something."

—Giunta addressing the attention he received due to the medal

Staff Sergeant Robert James Miller

MEDAL OF HONOR RECIPIENT 2010

Robert James Miller grew up in Wheaton, Illinois. He graduated high school in 2002 and enlisted as a Special Forces trainee on August 14, 2003. Miller first deployed to Afghanistan from August 2006 to March 2007 as part of Operation Enduring Freedom, and he returned in October 2007. While conducting operations in a village in Afghanistan, Miller was killed in combat with the Taliban. He posthumously received the Medal of Honor in 2010.

▼ *Staff Sgt. Robert J. Miller*

▼ *President Obama presents Miller's Medal of Honor to Miller's parents, Phillip and Maureen.*

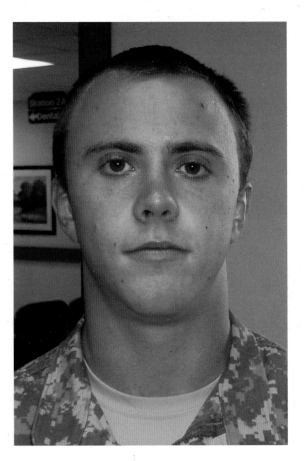

> "When the dust settled and the smoke cleared, there was no doubt Rob Miller and his team had struck a major blow against the local insurgency. Five members of his patrol had been wounded, but his team had survived. And one of his teammates surely spoke for all of them when he said of Rob, 'I would not be alive today if not for his ultimate sacrifice.'"
>
> —President Barack Obama

▲ *The breast star of the Order of Lincoln*

In January 2008, Miller was leading a team during a combat reconnaissance patrol in Kunar Province, Afghanistan. The team was attacked by 15–20 hidden insurgents firing heavy weapons. Miller initiated an assault on the fighters and called his command for air support. Despite the personal risk, he continued to fight while calling for his patrol to take cover in protected positions and allowing a wounded commander to be taken to safety. Miller was shot in the torso, but he refused to give up. He killed at least 10 insurgents and wounded many more, but he was mortally wounded in the process. He sacrificed his own life to save seven U.S. soldiers and 15 Afghanistan National Army soldiers.

President Barack Obama presented the Medal of Honor to Miller's parents on behalf of Robert on October 6, 2010. Miller was also given the highest honor in Illinois, the Order of Lincoln, in 2010. He was additionally inducted as a Laureate of The Lincoln Academy of Illinois.

Sergeant First Class Leroy A. Petry
MEDAL OF HONOR RECIPIENT 2011

Leroy Arthur Petry was born in Santa Fe, New Mexico, and joined the Army after graduating high school and spending a year studying at New Mexico Highlands University. He deployed several times to Iraq and Afghanistan and served in a number of positions such as grenadier, squad automatic rifleman, squad leader, and weapons squad leader. During his seventh deployment in May 2008, his heroic actions in the face of crippling injuries led him to become the second living recipient of the Medal of Honor for the War in Afghanistan.

On May 26, 2008, Perry and his unit were in Paktia Province, Afghanistan, on a mission to capture a high-value target from the Taliban. The unit came under strong fire from about 40 Taliban fighters. Petry was wounded in both legs, but was able to throw a thermobaric grenade from cover. A Taliban grenade then detonated near the

soldiers, wounding two of them. A second grenade landed near the men, and Petry picked it up to throw it in the opposite direction. However, the grenade detonated in the process and severed his right hand. It is likely that Petry's actions saved the other two soldiers from injury or death.

▲ *The Medal of Honor on Petry's uniform*

▶ *Petry is given a hero's welcome in his hometown of Santa Fe.*

Petry's right arm had to be amputated below the elbow due to his injuries from the battle. He now uses a prosthetic, on which a small plaque lists the names of the fallen Rangers of his regiment. Despite his injury, Petry deployed to Afghanistan once again and was promoted to sergeant first class. In 2010, Petry re-enlisted in the U.S. Army, but he decided to seek medical retirement in 2014, after nearly 15 years of service.

On July 12, 2011, President Barack Obama awarded Petry with the Medal of Honor.

Petry also holds several honors in his hometown of Santa Fe, including a nine-foot-tall statue of him that was unveiled at Santa Fe City Hall in 2013.

▼ *President Barack Obama and Sgt. First Class Leroy Petry make their way to the Medal of Honor presentation ceremony.*

"Every human impulse would tell someone to turn away. Every soldier is trained to seek cover. That's what Sergeant Leroy Petry could have done. Instead, this wounded Ranger, this 28-year-old man with his whole life ahead of him, this husband and father of four, did something extraordinary. He lunged forward, toward the live grenade. He picked it up... and threw it back— just as it exploded."

—President Barack Obama

Captain William Swenson

MEDAL OF HONOR RECIPIENT 2013

▲ *President Barack Obama presents Captain William Swenson with the Medal of Honor.*

▼ *Swenson is inducted into the Pentagon's Hall of Heroes.*

William D. Swenson, one of the only Medal of Honor recipients still on active duty, has deployed three times in the War on Terror. Swenson has been awarded the Bronze Star Medal (with two oak leaf clusters), the Purple Heart, and the Combat Infantryman Badge. Swenson's heroic actions during the 2009 Battle of Ganjgal in Afghanistan earned him the Medal of Honor in 2014.

While on his way to meet with village elders in Ganjgal and discuss improvements to a mosque, Swenson and his coalition force were ambushed by more than 60 insurgent fighters. A battle ensued for more than six hours. Swenson exhibited bravery in the face of battle by calling for air support and administering first aid to his wounded sergeant. He made several trips to the enemy's kill zone to aid the wounded, including four fallen U.S. servicemen.

On October 15, 2013, President Barack Obama awarded Swenson with the Medal of Honor. He became the first living officer to receive the Medal of Honor since Vietnam. He was also inducted into the Pentagon's Hall of Heroes in 2013.

> "The Battle of Ganjgal was ferocious. And it was tragic. And we lost so many good lives that day. But following the violence, and the death, came inspiration. And we were inspired by those who fought there, by those who would not accept defeat."
>
> —John M. McHugh, secretary of the Army

Staff Sergeant Ty Michael Carter

MEDAL OF HONOR RECIPIENT 2013

▲ *Ty Carter gives his statement to the press after receiving the Medal of Honor.*

▲ *President Barack Obama awards Staff Sergeant Ty Michael Carter with the Medal of Honor.*

Ty Michael Carter was born in Spokane, Washington, in 1980. He enlisted in the U.S. Marine Corps in October 1998 and the U.S. Army in January 2008. In May 2010, he was deployed to Afghanistan. His actions during the Battle of Kamdesh in 2009 earned him the Medal of Honor in 2013.

On October 3, 2009, Carter was stationed at Combat Outpost Keating when more than 300 enemy fighters attacked. Despite the threat of enemy fire, Carter twice crossed 100 meters of open ground to resupply ammunition. He also braved enemy machine gun fire to save a critically wounded comrade and provide first aid to the soldier, carrying him 30 meters to the Humvee. Carter suffered from severe wounds of his own while saving the lives of his fellow soldiers and protecting Combat Outpost Keating.

On August 26, 2013, President Barack Obama presented Staff Sergeant Ty Michael Carter with the Medal of Honor for his heroic actions. Carter was inducted into the Pentagon's Hall of Heroes the next day.

Carter left active duty in September 2014. He suffers from posttraumatic stress disorder and is currently working to destigmatize the condition.

Staff Sergeant Clinton L. Romesha

MEDAL OF HONOR RECIPIENT 2013

Clinton "Clint" Romesha was born into a family with a strong military background. His grandfather was a World War II veteran, his father was a Vietnam War veteran, and his two brothers were also in the military. Romesha joined the U.S. Army in 1999, and he has deployed to Kosovo, Iraq, and Afghanistan.

▼ *President Barack Obama awards Staff Sergeant Clinton L. Romesha with the Medal of Honor.*

▲ *Staff Sgt. Clint Romesha in Nuristan Province, Afghanistan*

▲ *Romesha is recognized during a ceremony at the Pentagon.*

Romesha was deployed to Afghanistan for Operation Enduring Freedom in May 2009 and assigned to Combat Outpost Keating. His actions during the Battle of Kamdesh earned him the Medal of Honor.

On October 3, 2009, around 300 Taliban fighters launched an attack on the outpost, wielding recoilless rifles, rocket-propelled grenades, mortars, machine guns, and small arms.

Taliban fighters fired on U.S. troops for three hours and then set fire to the compound. Despite the heavy fire, Romesha was able to move to seek reinforcements and organize a team of men to counterattack. Romesha took cover behind a generator, which was struck by a grenade, resulting in Romesha suffering shrapnel wounds to his neck, shoulder, and arms. Despite his wounds, Romesha succeeded in killing an estimated 30 Taliban while providing enough fire to allow other troops to regroup and fight. Eight American soldiers were killed in the costly 12-hour fight.

On February 11, 2013, President Barack Obama presented Romesha with the Medal of Honor. On February 12, he was inducted into the Pentagon's Hall of Heroes.

Romesha left the military in 2011 in order to spend more time with his wife and three children. He currently works in the oil industry in North Dakota. Romesha carries his Medal of Honor everywhere he goes.

"Throughout history, the question has often been asked, why? Why do those in uniform take such extraordinary risks? And what compels them to such courage? You ask Clint and any of these soldiers who are here today, and they'll tell you. Yes, they fight for their country, and they fight for our freedom. Yes, they fight to come home to their families. But most of all, they fight for each other, to keep each other safe and to have each other's backs."

—President Barack Obama

Corporal William "Kyle" Carpenter

MEDAL OF HONOR RECIPIENT 2014

William Kyle Carpenter was born in Jackson, Mississippi, in 1989 and enlisted in the Marine Corps' Delayed Entry Program at age 19.

Carpenter deployed to Helmand Province, Afghanistan, in support of Operation Enduring Freedom from September 2009 to November 2010.

On November 21, 2010, Carpenter and his team were fighting off a Taliban attack in a small village when Carpenter threw himself in front of a hand grenade to protect a fellow Marine. Carpenter suffered severe injuries to his face and arm, including the loss of his right eye and most of his teeth. He spent five weeks in a coma and more than two and a half years in the hospital, where he underwent nearly 40 surgeries.

Carpenter medically retired in 2013 and enrolled at the University of South Carolina in Columbia, where he earned a degree in international studies.

On June 19, 2014, President Barack Obama awarded Carpenter with the Medal of Honor.

> "Kyle is a shining example of what our nation needs to encourage—these veterans who come home and then use their incredible skills and talents to keep our country strong. And we can all learn from Kyle's example."
>
> —President Barack Obama

▶ *(Top right) Official photo of William Kyle Carpenter*

▶ *(Bottom right) President Barack Obama presents Carpenter with the Medal of Honor.*

Sergeant Kyle J. White
MEDAL OF HONOR RECIPIENT 2014

Kyle J. White enlisted in the U.S. Army in February 2006. In 2007, he was deployed to Aranas, Afghanistan, as part of Operation Enduring Freedom.

On November 9, 2007, White and his team were ambushed while trying to meet with village elders in Nuristan Province, Afghanistan. White was knocked unconscious after a grenade detonated near him. Upon waking, despite shrapnel wounds in his face and enemy fire raining down on him, White sprinted to assist a fellow wounded soldier and drag him to relative safety. White exposed himself to open fire several more times in order to save wounded soldiers. White then used his radio to report the situation.

White suffered multiple concussions during the attack, but continued to assist those who had been wounded. He only allowed himself to be evacuated once all of the other soldiers were brought to safety. White was later diagnosed with posttraumatic stress disorder.

On May 13, 2014, White was awarded the Medal of Honor by President Barack Obama. He was also inducted into the Pentagon's Hall of Heroes by Deputy Defense Secretary Robert O. Work.

▶ *President Barack Obama presents Sgt. Kyle White with the Medal of Honor.*

"During a long dark night, Spc. White's uncommon valor and perseverance saved lives and prevented the loss of U.S. bodies and equipment—Extraordinary and consistently selfless actions by a young paratrooper."

—Lt. Col William B. Ostlund, battalion commander, Task Force Rock, Feb. 20, 2008

Staff Sergeant Ryan Pitts

MEDAL OF HONOR RECIPIENT 2014

▲ *Staff Sergeant Ryan Pitts, April 2014*

In 2003, 17-year-old Ryan Pitts enlisted in the Army under the Delayed Entry Program. He initially decided to enlist as a way to pay for his college tuition. However, Pitts ended up not only putting his life on the line for his fellow soldiers, but earning a Medal of Honor in the process.

Pitts was nearing the end of his second tour in Afghanistan in July 2008 when he and 49 paratroopers were attacked by more than 200 enemy fighters. Pitts was knocked to the ground by a wave of grenades, and he sustained shrapnel wounds to his arms and legs. Despite bleeding heavily from the wounds, Pitts was able to return fire on the enemy, throwing grenades and releasing the safety lever on them to allow nearly immediate detonation. Pitts then put his own life at risk by whispering information to the Command Post, which was used to provide indirect fire support. Pitts's heroic actions prevented the enemy from overrunning post, capturing American soldiers, and attacking Wanat Vehicle Patrol Base.

"In Ryan Pitts you see the humility and the loyalty that define America's men and women in uniform. Of this medal, he says, It's not mine alone. It belongs to everybody who was there that day because we did it together."

—President Barack Obama

▲ *President Barack Obama awards Staff Sergeant Ryan Pitts with the Medal of Honor.*

▼ *Before Ryan Pitts is inducted into the Pentagon's Hall of Heroes, his wife straightens his medal.*

Pitts was medically retired due to his near-fatal wounds and was medically discharged from the Army in 2009.

On July 21, 2014, President Barack Obama awarded Pitts with the Medal of Honor, and he was additionally inducted into the Pentagon's Hall of Heroes. Pitts currently lives and works in New Hampshire with his son, Lucas.

"Despite life-threatening injuries—injuries that merited retreat from the [observation post]—he continued to fight."

—Then-Capt. Matthew Myer, company commander, Chosen Company, 2-503rd Inf. Regt. (from his official account of the events, written days after the battle)

Captain Florent Groberg

MEDAL OF HONOR RECIPIENT 2015

U.S. Army Captain Florent "Flo" Groberg was born in Poissy, France, in 1983 and moved to the United States when he was in middle school. After becoming a naturalized U.S. citizen in 2001, Groberg went on to attend the University of Maryland, College Park, graduating in 2006 with a bachelor's degree in criminology and criminal justice. In 2008, he joined the U.S. Army, where his heroic actions in Afghanistan earned him the Medal of Honor among numerous other awards and decorations.

On August 8, 2012, Groberg was serving as a personal security detachment (PSD) commander for Task Force Mountain Warrior. While traveling to a weekly security meeting in Asadabad, Kunar, Afghanistan, Groberg spotted a suspicious individual, who he soon realized was wearing a suicide vest. Groberg tackled the man. However, the individual proceeded to detonate the device, and Groberg went flying 15–20 feet away. A second suicide bomber was hidden nearby and detonated his own device. Four people were killed, and several others were injured.

▼ *Florent Groberg patrols Asadabad, Afghanistan, in February 2010.*

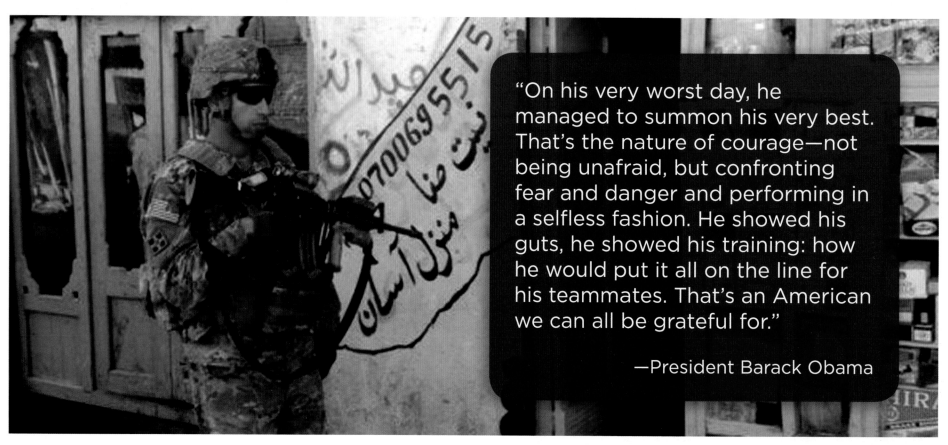

"On his very worst day, he managed to summon his very best. That's the nature of courage—not being unafraid, but confronting fear and danger and performing in a selfless fashion. He showed his guts, he showed his training: how he would put it all on the line for his teammates. That's an American we can all be grateful for."

—President Barack Obama

"Nothing can be accomplished without teamwork. I wouldn't be here without the incredible acts of my team."

—Retired Capt. Florent Groberg

Groberg sustained numerous injuries from the blast. He lost 45–50 percent of his left calf muscle and suffered from significant nerve damage, a blown eardrum, and a mild brain injury. However, Groberg's actions saved many lives. Groberg spent almost three years recovering at the Walter Reed National Military Medical Center, and he medically retired on July 23, 2015.

On November 12, 2015, President Barack Obama awarded Groberg with the Medal of Honor.

"The proudest thing I have ever done in my life is to wear this uniform and serve my country."

—Retired Capt. Florent Groberg

▲ *(Top left) U.S. Army Sgt. Andrew Mahoney (left) and Florent Groberg*

▲ *(Top right) President Barack Obama awards Capt. Florent Groberg with the Medal of Honor.*

▲ *(Bottom right) President Barack Obama and Capt. Groberg's family visit Groberg at Walter Reed National Medical Center in September 2012.*

Senior Chief Special Warfare Operator (SEAL) Edward C. Byers, Jr.

MEDAL OF HONOR RECIPIENT 2016

Edward C. Byers, Jr. was born in Toledo, Ohio. He enlisted in the U.S. Navy in 1998 and was assigned to his first SEAL team in May 2004. He served eleven overseas deployments, where his actions earned him five Bronze Stars and the Medal of Honor.

On December 5, 2012, an American physician named Dr. Dilip Joseph and two Afghans were captured by the Taliban. Military commanders gathered intelligence on the hostages' location, but feared that the hostages would be moved or killed in as few as four days.

On December 8, Byers and his unit hiked for more than four hours to reach the hostages. After the unit was spotted by an armed guard, Petty Officer Nicolas D. Checque sprinted toward the guard and killed him. Checque and Byers entered the compound, where Checque was immediately shot. Byers shot one Taliban fighter, straddled and killed an additional insurgent, and hurled himself on Dr. Joseph to keep him safe.

Byers attempted to resuscitate Checque without success, and Checque was posthumously awarded the Navy Cross.

On February 29, 2016, President Barack Obama awarded Edward Byers with the Medal of Honor. Byers is one of two Medal of Honor recipients serving on active duty as well as the most decorated living U.S. Navy Seal. Byers was promoted to senior chief petty officer in January 2016.

▶ *Official photo of Edward Byers*

▲ *Edward Byers and his family meet Secretary of Defense Ash Carter at the Pentagon.*

◄ *(Top left) President Barack Obama awards Edward Byers with the Medal of Honor.*

◄ *(Bottom left) Edward Byers, Jr.'s Medal of Honor*

"Like so many of our special operators, Ed is defined by a deep sense of humility. He doesn't seek the spotlight. In fact, he shuns it. He's the consummate quiet professional."

—President Barack Obama

Peter J. Ganci (FDNY Fire Chief)

HERO OF 9/11

Peter J. Ganci joined the New York City Fire Department in the 1960s after having served in the 32nd Airborne Division in the Vietnam War. During his career with the FDNY, Ganci was gradually promoted, and he eventually became Chief of Department.

Peter Ganci was tragically killed during the terrorist attacks of September 11, 2001, and he is remembered as a hero for being one of the first responders at the scene of the attack.

▼ *(Bottom left) A New York City firefighter looks out at the damage of 9/11.*

▼ *(Bottom right) New York City firefighters arrive at the scene of the 9/11 attacks.*

▲ *Peter Ganci's legacy lives on at the South Pool of the National September 11 Memorial & Museum.*

Ganci was on his way to court for jury duty when the first airplane hit the North Tower of the World Trade Center on September 11. Ganci got word of the crash and rushed to the scene, setting up a command post near the rubble of the fallen tower. Ganci and his team were allegedly in the basement of the South Tower when it collapsed after a second airplane crashed into it. However, they were able to dig themselves out of the rubble and set up a new command post, where they began directing people to safety.

While on the phone with Mayor Rudy Giuliani, Ganci told him that the North Tower looked like it would collapse as well, but he refused to evacuate the area himself. "I'm not leaving my men," he said. The North Tower collapsed, and Ganci was killed. His body was found under four feet of rubble.

Ganci's legacy lives on through several memorials, such as the Manas Air Base in Kyrgyzstan, unofficially known as Ganci Air Base, and the post office in Farmingdale, New York, which was named for him on Memorial Day, 2003.

Jason Thomas
HERO OF 9/11

Jason Thomas was a former United States Marine who heroically rescued people during the collapse of the World Trade Center on September 11. He also helped find a pair of Port Authority Police officers who had been stuck under the tower's rubble.

Thomas had previously served as a Marine during the War in Afghanistan and the Iraq War, but he left active duty in August 2001. He was on Long Island on the morning of September 11, 2001, when he got word that airplanes had struck the Twin Towers. Thomas put on his old Marines uniform and sped toward Manhattan.

After running into another former Marine, David Karnes, the pair began enlisting other soldiers and military members to start a search-and-rescue mission for people who may have been trapped under the rubble of the fallen buildings.

Despite being told that the mission was too dangerous, Thomas and the others braved hazards such as shards of metal and unstable mountains of debris, calling out for responses from people who had been buried. Finally, they heard a response and found two police officers.

▲ *Jason Thomas stands at the site of the September 11 attacks in his Marines uniform.*

► *Smoke billows from the Twin Towers after airplanes strike each of them during the deadliest terrorist attack in American history.*

Thomas returned to Ground Zero for many days after September 11 to offer his support and rescue efforts. He remained so humble about his mission that he did not even tell his five children about what he was doing.

In 2012, Thomas was living in Ohio and working as an officer for the Ohio Supreme Court, and as of 2013 he was serving as a medical technician in the United States Air Force.

"Someone needed help. It didn't matter who. I didn't even have a plan. But I have all this training as a Marine, and all I could think was, 'My city is in need.'"

—Jason Thomas

▼ *The rubble of the fallen towers at Ground Zero*

David Karnes

HERO OF 9/11

David Karnes was the former United States Marine who helped Jason Thomas with his rescue efforts following the September 11 attacks and the collapse of the World Trade Center.

Karnes had spent 23 years as a U.S. Marine but was working as an accountant in Connecticut when the attacks happened. After seeing the news coverage on television, Karnes put on his Marines uniform, gathered equipment, got a regulation haircut, stopped at his church to ask the pastor and parishioners to pray for him, and rushed to the scene to help.

Karnes sped to Manhattan going 120 miles per hour. Because of his uniform and haircut, he passed as a current member of the U.S. Military, and he was waved through the police barricades.

▼ *An aerial view of the World Trade Center after the September 11 attacks*

Once in Manhattan, Karnes ran into Jason Thomas, another former U.S. Marine, and the two men began searching the rubble for bodies. They navigated thick blankets of smoke and piles of rubble from the fallen buildings. After an hour of searching, they found two Port Authority officers, two of only 12 people who were pulled from the rubble alive. The officers were Will Jimeno and Sgt. John McLoughlin. They were 20 feet below the surface, where they remained trapped for 9 hours. It took three hours to pull out Jimeno and six more to rescue McLoughlin.

Karnes spent a total of 9 days helping with relief efforts, and he reenlisted in the Marine Corps Reserve when he returned home. He has since served in the Philippines and Iraq.

▼ *A fireman calls for more rescue workers to search for individuals trapped under the rubble.*

Welles Crowther
HERO OF 9/11

Welles Crowther was born in 1977 and raised in a New York City suburb, where he became a volunteer firefighter at age 16. In high school, he succeeded in academics and sports, and he eventually graduated from Boston College with a degree in economics. Crowther took a job as an equities trader in an office in the South Tower of the World Trade Center after graduating college.

On September 11, 2001, Crowther was evacuating the South Tower after the plane struck it. On his way out, he found a group of survivors. While carrying a badly burned woman on his back, Crowther directed the others to a stairwell and down to safety. He then ran back up to the 78th floor, where found another group of survivors whom he assisted to safety. He went back once again, but the South Tower collapsed while he was inside.

Crowther's body was not found until March 19, 2002. It is estimated that he saved the lives of up to 18 people in the attacks of September 11.

▼ *Welles Crowther's name on the South Pool of the National September 11 Memorial*

▼ *Smoke and fire emerge from the Twin Towers shortly before they each collapse. The ball of fire is coming from the South Tower, where Welles Crowther died.*

▲ *This photo of Bob Beckwith and George W. Bush thrust Beckwith into the public eye. The photo appeared on the cover of* Time *magazine.*

Bob Beckwith served with the New York City Fire Department for 30 years before retiring. On September 11, 2001, when Beckwith learned that a plane had struck the World Trade Center and saw the South Tower collapse on television, he rushed to Ground Zero. Wearing his old gear from his time working in the FDNY, he was able to get past the barricades. He began helping with rescue efforts, which included searching for people who had gone missing in the towers' collapses.

Beckwith was launched into national fame when a photo of him and President George W. Bush began circulating. He is currently very involved in fundraising for the New York Firefighters Burn Center Foundation.

Rick Rescorla

Born in Hayle, Cornwall, United Kingdom, in 1939, Rick Rescorla always dreamed of becoming a U.S. soldier. He joined the British military at age 17, and after becoming friends with an American soldier, Rescorla joined the U.S. Army. He was sent to Vietnam, where he received honors such as the Silver Star, Bronze Star with Oak Leaf Cluster, and Purple Heart.

After Vietnam, Rescorla attended college in Oklahoma, going on to get a law degree and teach criminal justice. He eventually took a job in corporate security, where his office was located in the World Trade Center in New York City.

Rescorla was convinced that the World Trade Center was not a safe place for his employees, and he even tried convincing his superiors to move the company to a safer location, such as New Jersey. Since they wouldn't move, Rescorla insisted that employees practice emergency evacuations every three months. He also implemented surprise fire drills and timed employees with a stopwatch to make sure they exited the building in a timely matter.

◄ *A memorial statue of Rick Rescorla along the Heritage Walk at the National Infantry Museum and Soldier Center*

▲ Rick Rescorla serving in Vietnam in 1965

On the morning of the September 11 attacks, Rescorla saw the first plane crash into the North Tower, and he ignored Port Authority's recommendation for employees in the South Tower to stay at their desks. He ordered an evacuation, and helped everyone remain calm even after the second plane crashed into the South Tower. Rescorla refused to evacuate the tower himself until he had gotten everybody else out.

Rescorla was last seen shortly before the tower collapsed, and his remains were never found.

Rick Rescorla is credited with saving the lives of almost 2,700 people on September 11. His diligent safety drills and ability to stay calm and take control under immense pressure make him a true hero.

▼ A memorial for Rescorla in his hometown of Hayle

▼ Rick Rescorla's name inscribed on a panel at the South Pool of the National September 11 Memorial.

The Rescue Dogs of September 11
HEROES OF 9/11

Almost 3,000 people were killed in the terrorist attacks on September 11, 2001, and over 6,000 more were injured when the North and South Towers of the World Trade Center collapsed.

Many people, both living and dead, were trapped under the rubble of the collapsed buildings, and thousands of rescue workers arrived on the scene to search for them, including more than 300 rescue dogs.

The dogs scoured the rubble for survivors, since they had been trained to detect the scent of living humans. As time went on and the likelihood of finding survivors diminished, the dogs were also used to detect dead bodies and human remains that had been buried. Some dogs worked shifts of up to 12 hours long, despite dangerous conditions and the mental exhaustion that came from finding very few survivors.

When it became clear that the dogs could not find any more people, dead or alive, they became comfort dogs for firefighters and other rescue workers who were mentally drained from their own search efforts.

◄ *A dog is removed from the debris at Ground Zero.*

One of the most famous rescue dogs of September 11 was Bretagne, a golden retriever who worked at Ground Zero for 10 days. After aiding in the September 11 rescue efforts, she went on to work in rescue missions during Hurricanes Katrina, Rita, and Ivan.

Another rescue dog, Apollo, was the first to arrive after the collapse of the Twin Towers. He was almost killed by falling and burning debris. Unfazed, he continued his rescue work as though nothing had happened.

Rescue dogs are credited with saving dozens of survivors in the attacks.

▶ *Apollo the rescue dog at Ground Zero*

▼ *A statue in New Jersey commemorating the contribution of rescue dogs to the 9/11 rescue efforts*

Captain Chesley Sullenberger

EVERYDAY HERO

Born near an Air Force base in Texas in 1951, Chesley Sullenberger showed an interest in airplanes and aircraft from a young age. Excelling in high school academics, Sullenberger went on to get a Bachelor of Science from the United States Air Force Academy and master's degrees from Purdue University and the University of Northern Colorado.

Upon graduating from the United States Air Force Academy, Sullenberger was awarded the Outstanding Cadet in Airmanship award. He earned his wings in 1975 and went on to fly as a fighter pilot for the U.S. Air Force in the United Kingdom. He attained the rank of captain while in the Air Force, and he also served as a member of an investigation board for aircraft accidents.

Sullenberger worked for U.S. Airways from 1980–2010, and he founded Safety Reliability Methods, Inc. in 2007, which provides guidance for airplane safety, performance, and reliability.

▶ *Sullenberger's Air Force Academy yearbook photo*

Sullenberger's most memorable and heroic actions took place on January 15, 2009. While piloting an Airbus A320, his plane struck a flock of geese. The collision caused both engines to lose power, and Sullenberger was forced to make an emergency water landing on the Hudson River. Everyone on the plane survived the landing, and they were rescued by boats. Sullenberger did not leave the aircraft until he was sure all passengers and crew had been evacuated.

Sullenberger's actions were honored and recognized by President George W. Bush, President-elect Barack Obama, the United States Senate, and the United States House of Representatives. Additionally, Sullenberger was presented with the Medal of Valor by Chief Richard Price of the San Ramon Valley Fire Protection District, as well as the Founder's Medal by The Air League.

In 2016, a biographical film called *Sully* was made about Sullenberger's life and heroic actions. It was met with positive reviews and nominated for numerous awards.

▶ *(Top right) Chesley Sullenberger and his wife, Lorrie*

▶ *(Bottom right) The engine from U.S. Airways Flight 1549 is lifted out of the Hudson River.*

Captain Richard Phillips
EVERYDAY HERO

Richard Phillips was born in Massachusetts in 1955 and graduated from the Massachusetts Maritime Academy in 1979. As captain of the *Maersk Alabama* in 2009, Phillips was taken hostage by Somali pirates, and he is recognized as a hero for the selflessness and concern he showed for the safety of his crew.

On April 8, 2009, the *Maersk Alabama* was sailing from Salalah, Oman, to Mombasa, Kenya. It had a crew of 20 and was carrying cargo and relief supplies to be delivered to Kenya, Somalia, and Uganda. While located about 300 nautical miles off the coast of Eyl, a Somalian port city, Phillips' ship was hijacked by four Somali pirates.

▶ *Richard Phillips at the premier of* Captain Phillips, *a movie based on the Somali pirate hostage situation.*

▼ *The* Maersk Alabama

▲ *A military ship patrols the ocean for pirates and terrorists.*

▶ *(Top right) Captain Phillips (right) after being rescued*

▶ *(Bottom right) Richard Phillips is presented with the Admiral Arleigh Burke Leadership Award.*

The crew members locked themselves in the engine room while the pirates boarded the ship, but Phillips offered himself as a hostage. He was taken onto a small life boat by the pirates, who repeatedly threatened to kill him. He made one attempt to escape by jumping into the sea, but he was recaptured.

On Sunday, April 12, Navy snipers killed three of the pirates after seeing they had Phillips tied up with a gun pointed to his head. Phillips was saved. He credits those Navy Seals as the real heroes of his story, but the courage he showed under pressure and the sacrifice he made for his crew make him a hero nonetheless.

Staff Sergeant Spencer Stone, Specialist Alek Skarlatos, and Anthony Sadler

EVERYDAY HEROES

On August 21, 2015, three young Americans—Staff Sergeant Spencer Stone, Specialist Alek Skarlatos, and Anthony Sadler—were on a train traveling from Amsterdam to Paris. Suddenly, a 25-year-old man named Ayoub El Khazzani began to open fire on the train's passengers with an AKM assault rifle. Two French men tried to stop Khazzani, but one fell to the floor during the struggle, and the other was shot in the back by a second concealed weapon that Khazzani had been carrying. The man was not killed, but he played dead so he would not get shot again.

Khazzani entered the passenger car, but his rifle jammed. While he was trying to clear the rifle, Stone, Skarlatos, and Sadler tackled him. They put him in a chokehold and beat him with his own rifle. Khazzani cut Stone with a boxcutter and nearly severed his thumb, but the gunman was beaten unconscious and held down with his arms tied behind his back.

▼ *(Bottom left) Skarlatos, Stone, and Sadler with French president Francois Hollande and Jane Hartley, United States Ambassador to France*

▼ *(Bottom right) Spencer Stone*

▲ *(Top left) Skarlatos, Sadler, and Stone at the premiere of* The 15:17 to Paris, *the film based on their heroic actions*

▲ *(Top right) Alek Skarlatos with Francois Hollande and Jane Hartley*

Skarlatos searched for more gunmen on the train while Stone provided medical care for the man who had been shot. The train was rerouted to Arras, and the remaining passengers were searched before being allowed to go to Paris.

In the following investigation, it was found that the gunman's internet history showed terrorist intent. Additionally, Spanish authorities knew him to be involved with drug trafficking.

The three American men who stopped Khazzani were hailed as heroes by the French Preisdent, the British Prime Minister, and American President Barack Obama. Sadler was awarded the Secretary of Defense Medal of Valor, Skarlatos was awarded the Soldier's Medal, and Stone was awarded the Airman's Medal.

Sergeant Kimberly Munley
EVERYDAY HERO

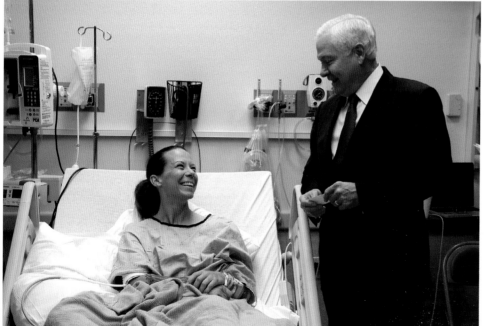

In November 2009, at a military base in Fort Hood, Texas, Sgt. Kimberly Munley spotted a gunman chasing and trying to shoot an already-wounded soldier. The gunman was later identified as Maj. Nidal Malik Hasan, and he was going on a deadly shooting rampage at the military base.

Kimberly Munley, a 34-year-old former soldier who was at the time serving as a member of Fort Hood's civilian police department, was working traffic patrol duty when she heard the first shots of Hasan's rampage.

Munley headed toward the sound of the gunfire and engaged the man in a shoot-off. She shot at Hasan, which prompted him to charge at her while both individuals continued firing at one another. Hasan was eventually shot down. Munley sustained injuries to both thighs as well as her wrist. She had to undergo two surgeries, since one of the bullets hit an artery, but she ultimately survived the wounds.

◄ *(Top left) President Barack Obama congratulates Sgt. Kimberly Munley for her service and bravery.*

◄ *(Bottom left) Robert M. Gates, Defense Secretary, visits an injured Munley at the hospital.*

Ever since the beginning of her career as a police officer, Munley was known for her fearlessness, and she had a reputation for chasing down burglars and gunmen. According to her family, police work is her true calling.

Munley put her extensive training to use in the gunman situation, and her quick thinking and tremendous courage saved an unknowable number of lives that day.

▼ *Kimberly Munley is awarded a medal by Chief of Staff of the U.S. Army, Gen. George W. Casey Jr.*

Lassana Bathily

EVERYDAY HERO

Lassana Bathily was a 24-year old undocumented immigrant living in Paris in 2015, where he worked stacking shelves at a supermarket. One day while he was at work, a gunman entered his store, shooting and killing four people.

Bathily was downstairs in the stockroom when he heard the gunshots, and he noticed customers running down the stairs. The gunman, Amedy Coulibaly, had taken several of the supermarket's customers hostage, and he began to demand more hostages.

Bathily ushered the customers who had run downstairs to safety while he exited through the fire escape and spoke with the police officers who were waiting outside. Bathily coordinated with the police to come up with a plan to save the hostages. After several hours of planning, the police raided the store, where they shot and killed Coulibaly. Coulibaly had killed nine Jewish hostages before the police were able to stop him.

▼ *Lassana Bathily (middle) attends a ceremony honoring his courageous acts.*

▲ *A memorial outside the supermarket for the hostages killed by Coulibaly*

▲ *People line up outside the Hyper Cacher supermarket to pay tribute to the victims of the hostage situation.*

▼ *Police officers guard the Eiffel Tower after the series of terrorist attacks in Paris in 2015.*

Bathily's story served as a ray of hope in Paris's tumultuous political climate of 2015. Over the course of three days in 2015, 17 people were killed in Paris in a series of terrorist attacks.

Bathily, who had been living in France for nine years and struggling to gain citizenship, was granted French citizenship by French president Francois Hollande after his actions. He remained humble upon being called a hero.

Micah Fletcher

EVERYDAY HERO

In May 2017 on a MAX Light Rail train in Portland, Oregon, a 35-year old passenger named Jeremy Joseph Christian began shouting anti-Muslim and racist slurs at two young women on the train. One of the women was a 17-year old Muslim woman wearing a hijab, and the second was a 16-year old black woman. The man shouted at them to "go back to Saudi Arabia" and even told them to kill themselves.

Three other passengers began to confront the man, asking him to leave the train, but he stabbed all three of them. A U.S. Army veteran and father of four named John Best and a recent university graduate named Taliesin Myrddin Namkai-Meche both died in the attack. Micah Fletcher, the third man who confronted the suspect, survived despite serious knife wounds to the neck.

Jeremy Christian, a white nationalist, was arrested and charged with murder and attempted murder, among other crimes.

► *(Top right) Micah Fletcher prepares to talk to the leader of the extremist group that Jeremy Christian may have had contact with.*

► *(Bottom right) A MAX Light Rail train*

After the attack, Fletcher spoke out publicly in support of the families of the men who had been killed. He also spoke on behalf of the two teenagers whom Christian was targeting in his hateful tirade. Fletcher pointed out that these young women were also victims of the attack.

He went on to become involved in local politics, using his newfound status as a hero to call for the community of Portland to focus more on political activism and protecting one another as citizens of a shared city. Some topics that he focused on during his involvement in politics were finding more humane ways to resolve the city's housing crisis and speaking out against social injustices against Muslims.

The attack brought to national attention the rise of hate speech and Islamophobia in the United States.

▼ *A vigil for the two men who were killed by Jeremy Christian on the MAX Light Rail train*

Petty Officer First Class Anthony Mugavero

EVERYDAY HERO

Around Christmas 2017 in Guam, Navy Petty Officer 1st Class Anthony Mugavero was in the parking garage of the Micronesia Mall with his family when they began hearing shouts from a woman that her purse had been stolen.

Mugavero spotted the suspect and ran after him, jumping over a wall and tackling him. After a physical altercation with the man, Mugavero retrieved the woman's purse. The suspect fled, and the woman got her purse back. Since he didn't know whether or not the purse-snatcher was armed, Mugavero did not pursue him any further.

On December 29, 2017, Mugavero received a legislative resolution and certificate of recognition for his actions. He also spoke out saying he hoped his story would work to help foster relationships between the citizens of Guam and the military presence on the island.

▼ *Guam Sen. Dennis Rodriguez Jr. presents Navy Petty Officer 1st Class Anthony Mugavero with a legislative resolution.*

Aitzaz Hasan

EVERYDAY HERO

In January 2014, Aitzaz Hasan, a 15-year old student from Pakistan, was outside his high school with a few other classmates, forbidden from attending a school assembly due to tardiness.

The students noticed a man in his twenties approaching the school. Aitzaz's friends ran inside upon seeing that the man was wearing a detonator on his vest, but despite their objections, Aitzaz approached and confronted the man. He would not let the man go inside and kill his friends. The man detonated his vest, killing Aitzas and himself, but no one else was harmed. It was estimated that around 2,000 students were inside the school at the time.

Aitzaz became known as a hero throughout Pakistan for risking his life to save so many of his friends and classmates. Public officials throughout the country applauded his bravery, and he was posthumously given a Global Bravery Award by the International Human Rights commission.

▲ *Aitzaz Hasan*

▼ *Students protest Taliban attacks in Pakistan. Aitzaz was a vocal critic of the group, since a number of Shia Muslims in his area were killed by the Taliban.*

Cory Harris, Frances Rush, Michael Burns, and MTA officers

EVERYDAY HEROES

On January 23, 2015, at Grand Central Station in New York City, a 70-year-old man visiting from Kentucky suddenly collapsed. The man, Moises Dreszer, had gone into cardiac arrest. Several strangers then came together to save his life.

As Dreszer's wife yelled for someone to call 911, an MTA Assistant Station Manager, Cory Harris, saw what had happened and called Fire Command. He went on to check Dreszer's vital signs while they waited for more assistance

Another bystander, 27-year-old Frances Rush, happened to be a trained EMT, and he began performing CPR on Dreszer. Meanwhile Michael Burns, an MTA Police Officer, found a defibrillator. The men used the defibrillator to restore Dreszer's pulse after two shocks.

Emergency personnel arrived, and Dreszer was taken to the hospital, where he was stabilized. He was released five days later in good condition. Dreszer's wife believes that had these men not helped her husband, he would likely have died.

► *(Top right) Grand Central Station, where Dreszer suffered cardiac arrest*

► *(Bottom right) MTA employees visit Moises Dreszer at the hospital.*

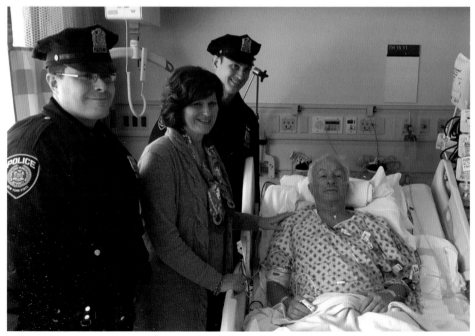

David Jensen

EVERYDAY HERO

▲ *David Jensen receives the Secretary of Defense Medal of Valor.*

David Jensen was a contractor from South Dakota who served with the U.S. Army as an Operational Advisor in Afghanistan in 2012.

On September 10, 2012, Jensen and his team were preparing for an air assault, when a rocket set off by enemy fighters hit one of their aircraft.

Jensen evacuated the men from the aircraft, despite the fact that it could potentially catch on fire at any moment. He went back to the aircraft several more times to rescue a total of four paratroopers. The aircraft burst into flames after Jensen had removed all of the men. Jensen then administered medical aid to the wounded soldiers.

Jensen was awarded the Office of the Secretary of Defense Medal for Valor at the Pentagon Hall of Heroes for his actions. This medal recognizes heroic government employees or private citizens who risk their own lives in order to save the lives of others.

Officer Jason Salas, Officer Robert Sparks, and Captain Raymond Bottenfield

MEDAL OF VALOR RECIPIENTS

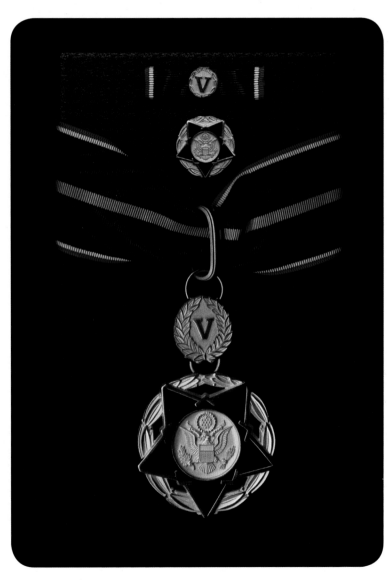

▲ *The Medal of Valor*

On June 7, 2013, a gunman went on a deadly shooting rampage through Santa Monica, California. The gunman, 23-year-old John Zawahri, had killed several of his family members, set fire to his family's home, and was randomly shooting and killing people in the streets of Santa Monica. He made his way toward the campus of Santa Monica College, shooting at cars in the parking lot, campus police officers, and random bystanders. He then entered the school's library, continuing to fire.

Officer Robert Sparks, Officer Jason Salas, and Santa Monica College Police Captain Ray Bottenfield rushed toward the sound of gunfire. As students ran out of the library in hysterics about the violent gunman inside, the three officers ran inside toward the danger. They yelled at Zawahri to drop his weapon, which he had pointed at a student on the ground.

Instead of dropping his rifle, Zawahri began shooting at the officers, who fired right back. They eventually killed him in the shoot-out.

Zawahri killed a total of five people in his rampage, including his own father and brother, as well as an elderly woman known to walk around Santa Monica College's campus collecting cans for her church group.

Later that month, President Barack Obama presented Salas, Sparks, and Bottenfield with the Medal of Valor for of their heroic actions in stopping the shooting spree. They likely saved many lives, while putting their own lives in grave danger. The Medal of Valor is the nation's highest honor for public safety officers.

▼ *President Barack Obama awards Officer Robert Sparks with the Medal of Valor. Captain Ray Bottenfield can be seen on the left, and Officer Jason Salas on the right.*

"Each of them will tell you very humbly the same thing: They were just doing their jobs. They were doing what they had to do, what they were trained to do, like on any other day."

—President Barack Obama at the Medal of Valor ceremony for Sparks, Salas, and Bottenfield

Deputy Jennifer Fulford-Salvano

MEDAL OF VALOR RECIPIENT

On May 5, 2004, Jennifer Fulford-Salvano was on patrol with a trainee in Orange County, Florida, when they received a call from a young child, saying that there were strangers in his home. They went to the address that the child gave them, where a woman on the lawn proceeded to tell them that there were three strange men inside her house. She could not provide a reason why.

Unbeknownst to the officers, the woman had hundreds of pounds of marijuana hidden in her garage and $60,000 in cash hidden in her home. The men were there to rob her.

▼ *Vice President Dick Cheney awards Jennifer Fulford-Salvano with the Medal of Valor in 2005.*

▲ *The Orange County, Florida, Sheriff's Office*

Gesturing to the open garage, the woman started crying that her children were in the minivan parked inside of it. While other officers searched the exterior of the home, Fulford-Salvano was focused on saving the children. Entering the garage and looking into the van, she saw two-year-old twins and the young boy who had placed the phone call, but she could not open the locked door.

Someone in the house began firing shots and then entered the garage. He noticed Fulford-Salvano and proceeded to fire at her. She fired back at him until he collapsed against the wall.

A second man began firing at Fulford-Salvano, and just as she shot at him, she was hit in the right shoulder. She successfully shot both of the men in their heads, but had to stay on guard and continue to protect herself, despite the enormous amount of blood she was losing from her wounds. She focused on keeping herself alive. Other officers on the scene then pulled her from the garage and rushed her to the hospital in an ambulance. It was discovered later that she had been hit by ten bullets.

The two men Fulford-Salvano had shot in the head both died, a third man in the house received a sentence of life in prison, and the woman and her husband occupying the house both went to jail for drug trafficking.

In July of 2005, Fulford-Salvano was awarded the Medal of Valor by Vice President Dick Cheney for her heroic efforts in saving the trapped children and engaging in a shoot-off with dangerous criminals.

Officer Rodney Lee Chambers

MEDAL OF VALOR RECIPIENT

In June 2003, at Union Station in Washington, D.C., Officer Rodney Lee Chambers was on patrol when he began receiving reports that a man had been spotted with a grenade. Officer Chambers located the man, stopped him, and grabbed the grenade from him. Chambers squeezed the grenade to prevent it from detonating. He then waited for 20 minutes for a bomb disposal team to come and take care of the device safely and professionally.

It was eventually determined that the grenade was not functional, but that was not known to Chambers when he grabbed it. Chambers still risked his own life and risked a grenade going off in his own hands for the safety of the travelers at Union Station.

Because he placed his own life in danger for the safety of the civilians at the station, Officer Chambers was awarded the Medal of Valor by Vice President Dick Cheney on July 14, 2005.

◄ *(Top left) Vice President Dick Cheney awards Officer Rodney Lee Chambers with the Medal of Valor.*

◄ *(Bottom left) Union Station in Washington, D.C., where officer Chambers bravely stopped a man with a grenade*

Officer Reeshemah Taylor

MEDAL OF VALOR RECIPIENT

▲ *Vice President Joe Biden and Officer Reeshemah Taylor at the Medal of Valor ceremony*

In 2009, Officer Reeshemah Taylor was working in the Medical Unit of Osceola County Jail in Florida when one of her colleagues went mysteriously missing. It was soon discovered that a violent inmate had taken the colleague hostage and stolen his uniform. This inmate, a gang member with three life sentences and no parole, was planning to escape from the jail while dressed as an officer. He was armed with a gun and likely ready to shoot at anyone trying to get in his way.

While searching for her colleague, Officer Taylor came face to face with the inmate, who pointed the gun right at her. She swiftly grabbed the gun while kneeing the man and putting him in a headlock. Taylor was able to use her free hand to use her radio and call for assistance.

If not for Taylor's quick thinking and bravery under pressure, the inmate would have likely succeeded in his plan to escape, and could have killed many people.

Taylor was awarded the Medal of Valor for her actions.

Staff Sergeant Jeremiah Workman

BRONZE STAR RECIPIENT

Jeremiah Workman grew up in Marion, Ohio, and enlisted in the U.S. Marine Corps shortly after his 17th birthday. He had always longed to be an Ohio state trooper, but he was not old enough. He decided instead to join the Marines and remain in service until he was 21.

In 2004, Workman was sent to a base outside of Fallujah, Iraq, one of the most dangerous places to be stationed. In November of that year, his platoon received orders for Operation Phantom Fury—a plan to attack Fallujah. They attacked the city for 17 days before being sent to search the city's houses for weapons.

While searching a home, Workman and his men encountered a group of insurgents. Workman ordered men to guard the house from insurgent gunfire, and he led more men inside. They were then informed that there were Marines stuck inside the house with the insurgents.

▼ *Vice President Joe Biden presents Staff Sgt. Jeremiah Workman with the Bronze Star.*

▲ *United States Marines in Fallujah, Iraq*

Workman and his team encountered heavy gunfire and the threat of grenades once inside the house. Two of the Marines trapped in the house had already been killed by the time Workman and his team got to them. Workman was able to carry a third wounded Marine to safety.

Workman and his team stormed back into the house, seeking vengeance for their fallen fellow Marines. They encountered yet another grenade, and one Marine even had part of his arm ripped off by an AK47. The Marines lost three men in the altercation, but succeeded in killing 24 insurgents.

Workman and his platoon remained in Fallujah until April 2005. Upon returning to the United States, Workman experienced mental trauma from his time spent in Iraq. He was then diagnosed with post-traumatic stress disorder.

In 2006, Workman received the Navy Cross for his bravery. In 2011, Vice President Joe Biden presented him with a Bronze Star. However, Workman rejects being called a hero, and he feels guilt and responsibility for the deaths of the Marines in Fallujah.

Captain Simratpal Singh
BRONZE STAR RECIPIENT

Simratpal Singh was born in Punjab, India, and immigrated to California with his family when he was a child. Singh had always had a fascination with the U.S. Army and admired the ideals promoted by the Army, particularly standing up for those who cannot defend themselves.

Singh, a member of the Sikh faith, attended West Point in 2006, a time when Sikhs were not allowed to practice their religion in the military. Despite his turban, long hair, and beard, all Sikh symbols to represent a commitment to service and justice, Singh decided to adhere to the military's standards of appearance. He shaved his beard, cut his hair, and stopped wearing a turban.

Singh graduated from West Point in 2010, and he went on to serve as a platoon leader in Afghanistan during Operation Enduring Freedom. He earned a Bronze Star for leading a team to clear explosive devices while in Afghanistan. He went on to oversee a multi-million dollar budget as a Brigade Comptroller, and was continuously praised as a phenomenal worker by his superiors. He then received a master's degree in engineering.

Captain Singh is known for being the first active duty member of the military to seek

▲ *A traditional Sikh beard and turban*

▲ *A Sikh soldier in the U.S. Army*

an accommodation for his religion-influenced appearance. He requested a special accommodation from the Army to wear a turban over his long hair and to keep his long beard. Because of this, he has been commended for standing up for what's right in the face of difficulty and for bringing greater attitudes of religious tolerance to the U.S. military. He has since assisted in helping other members of the Sikh faith integrate their articles of faith into their own military service.

In 2016, a federal court ruled in favor of Captain Singh, allowing him religious accommodation for the entirety of his military career. What may seem like one small step is, in actuality, paving the way for greater religious acceptance in the Army.

> "I am thankful that I no longer have to make the choice between faith and service to our nation."
>
> —Captain Simratpal Singh

▼ *A Sikh soldier completes his officer training while keeping his hair, beard, and turban. Captain Singh's efforts helped make this possible.*

Petty Officer Nathan Bruckenthal

BRONZE STAR RECIPIENT

Nathan Bruckenthal was born in Stony Brook, New York, in 1979. He and his family lived in many different places, including Hawaii, Virginia, and Connecticut, and Bruckenthal even served as a volunteer firefighter while living in Connecticut. He joined the U.S. Coast Guard in 1999, and intended to go to college and become a police officer or firefighter after his time in the service.

While in the Coast Guard, Bruckenthal deployed twice to the Persian Gulf. During his first deployment, he was awarded both the Armed Forces Expeditionary Medal and the Combat Action Ribbon.

During his second tour in 2004, while intercepting an Arabian vessel carrying out a waterborne attack on the Khawr Al Amaya Oil Terminal, Bruckenthan and two Navy petty officers were killed in the boat's explosion. Because of the explosion, security forces were able to locate the area of the attack and destroy two more vessels carrying explosives. Many lives were saved and casualties prevented because of this.

After his death, Bruckenthal was awarded the Bronze Star, the Purple Heart, and the Global War on Terrorism Expeditionary Medal.

◄ *A photo of Nathan Bruckenthal*

▼ *Bruckenthal's parents display a photo of their son at a memorial service.*

Staff Sergeant Katteri Franklin

BRONZE STAR RECIPIENT

Katteri Franklin always knew that she wanted to spend her life helping others, and she intended to become a police officer some day. Instead, her career took her into more than 10 years of service in the U.S. military, where her desire to help others made itself clear.

One example of her selflessness occurred while she was deployed in Iraq in 2007. Franklin encountered an Iraqi man with a bullet in his head and one eye dangling from its socket. She bandaged the man and helped him to the best of her ability.

Another time, Franklin encountered a soldier with two chest wounds. She pushed other soldiers out of the way and attended to his wounds herself.

While in Iraq, Franklin also worked closely with women and children civilians. As a female member of the U.S. Army, the women seemed to trust her more, and in return, Franklin made sure they received proper medical aid and treatment.

Franklin received a Bronze Star for having "contributed greatly to the survival of the wounded." However, Franklin does not consider herself a hero—she's just doing her job. She hopes that her actions can serve as an example to younger soldiers.

▲ *Katteri Franklin*

Major F. Damon Friedman

BRONZE STAR RECIPIENT

Damon Friedman joined the Marines in 2000 and then transferred to the Air Force Spec Ops. He deployed four different times, to both Iraq and Afghanistan.

In April of 2010, Major F. Damon Friedman was assigned to an Army task force while serving as an Air Force Special Operations Command special tactics officer in Afghanistan. While in the Korengal Valley of Afghanistan, also known as the "Valley of Death," Friedman was appointed to lead an attack on enemy forces in the middle of the night.

Stationed at an elevated point in the valley, Friedman used his position to fire at the enemy forces below him while his men moved through the valley. He also conducted the aircraft providing vital support to the valley. Friedman exposed himself to enemy fire several times in order to direct the aircraft.

None of Friedman's men were killed during the seven days he directed air support, but 40 enemies were killed or wounded, all credited to Friedman's efforts.

In 2013, Friedman was awarded a Bronze Star with Valor for his actions in Afghanistan.

◀ *(Top left) Friedman (right) with his wife and son after receiving the Bronze Star medal with Valor in 2013*

◀ *(Bottom left) Friedman's son hold's his father's Bronze Star medal.*

Sergeant Monica Beltran

BRONZE STAR RECIPIENT

Sgt. Monica Beltran was from Woodbridge, Virginia, and joined the Virginia National Guard as a high school senior. In 2004, she deployed to Iraq for Operation Iraqi Freedom. While serving gun turret duty, she often faced backlash for being a young woman. Her male peers were uncomfortable with serving in combat alongside a woman.

In 2005, 55 soldiers were being transported to a new operating base, and Beltran was in charge of providing security for them. The convoy came under enemy attack, but Beltran proceeded to fire back, not even stopping when her hand was wounded. She provided protection for her convoy for the entirety of the mile-long kill zone.

On December 30, 2005, Beltran became the first woman in the Virginia National Guard to be awarded the Bronze Star Medal for Valor.

▼ *Beltran is honored at a Virginia Women in History event.*

▼ *Sgt. Monica Beltran*

Captain Gregory Ambrosia

SILVER STAR RECIPIENT

Gregory Ambrosia was born in Indianapolis, Indiana, in 1982, and graduated from the U.S. Military Academy at West Point in 2005.

In September of 2007, Ambrosia was stationed in Afghanistan at the Korengal Outpost. The terrain surrounding the outpost was very rugged and dangerous, and Ambrosia and his team had little contact with the outside world while stationed there.

On the night of September 27, Ambrosia and his men were stationed at a makeshift outpost. Enemy fighters began an assault on the troopers, but the troopers were unable to figure out where the gunfire was coming from. The enemy began closing in on them, getting close enough to throw grenades. Since the enemy was so close, Ambrosia was forced to call for his own men to shoot at his own position.

Their vision was quickly blocked by smoke, and their request for support would not arrive for 45 minutes. The enemy fighters began to use their hand grenades, but Ambrosia and his men repelled the fighters until a helicopter arrived. Two of his men were wounded, but none were killed.

Ambrosia was presented with the Silver Star for the leadership he took during the dangerous, life-threatening situation. Had he not acted valiantly in the face of danger, many more of his men could have been injured, or even killed.

▶ *Army Capt. Gregory Ambrosia receives the Silver Star.*

Sergeant First Class Ryan A. Ahern and Captain Tom Bozzay

SILVER STAR RECIPIENTS

Sgt. First Class Ryan Ahern and Army Capt. Tom Bozzay were stationed in Afghanistan in 2009. In December of that year, they were both part of a team protecting a French military unit when they came under attack from an enemy force. Five members of the unit were seriously injured, and Bozzay, completely disregarding his own safety, moved through a barrage of enemy fire in order to provide care for them. He even used his body as a shield to protect the wounded soldiers from the gunfire.

Ahern was knocked unconscious when the attack initially started, but upon regaining consciousness, he identified where the attack was coming from and immediately fired back at the enemy. This allowed the other members of his unit to get back to their positions and continue to fight.

Both Ahern and Bozzay were awarded the Silver Star Medal for their actions during the battle.

◄ *Tom Bozzay is awarded the Silver Star.*

▼ *Ryan Ahern accepts the Silver Star medal.*

Specialist Monica Lin Brown

SILVER STAR RECIPIENT

Army Spc. Monica Lin Brown was from Lake Jackson, Texas, and was serving as an Army medic in the Paktia Province of Afghanistan by the time she was just 18-years-old.

In April 2007, a vehicle in Brown's convoy was hit with a bomb. Since springtime was the time of year when the Taliban would re-enter Afghanistan after staying in Pakistan for the winter, it was known as a particularly dangerous season when fighting often started back up.

After the vehicle had been hit, Brown and her team began noticing fire all around them. They approached the burning vehicle, and Brown saw that all five people who had been inside of it were injured, two critically. Brown pulled the soldiers to a safer location, despite fire and shrapnel raining down on them. She used her own body to shield her wounded fellow soldiers, and she was able to treat the wounded soldiers on site before getting them into a helicopter to be taken to a safer location.

◄ *Vice President Dick Cheney presents Spc. Monica Lin Brown with the Silver Star.*

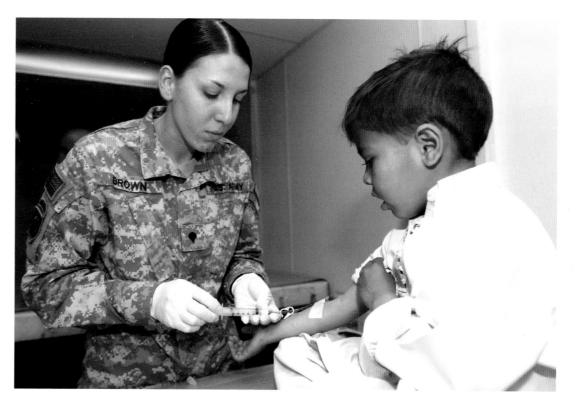

▲ *Spc. Monica Lin Brown helps a young Afghan boy.*

◄ *Spc. Monica Lin Brown on duty*

Brown was awarded the Silver Star for her actions that day and for her bravery while in the line of duty. Her winning the medal was significant, as she was only the second woman since World War II to receive it.

Also significantly, the Pentagon's policy normally does not allow women to serve in frontline combat roles. However, the wars in Afghanistan and Iraq did not have clear front lines, allowing women soldiers to play a larger role in combat than they had in previous wars. Brown's Silver Star was a victory not only for the U.S. Army, but for all women soldiers.

Staff Sergeant Daniel W. Ridgeway

SILVER STAR RECIPIENT

On June 18, 2011, Staff Sgt. Daniel Ridgeway was serving on his third deployment. He was deployed to Helmand province in Afghanistan, one of the deadliest areas for Coalition Forces. Ridgeway himself even said that somebody stationed there was seriously injured or killed every two weeks.

Ridgeway encountered explosives on two separate patrols that day. During the first patrol, the Marines were walking in a single file line heading toward a weapons cache and staying alert for explosives being

▶ *A color guard stands during the Silver Star Medal award ceremony for Sgt. Daniel Ridgeway.*

▼ *Daniel Ridgeway receives the Silver Star medal.*

▲ *Marines and soldiers in attendance at Ridgeway's Silver Star Medal Ceremony*

used in a land mine-like manner. Each Marine stepped into the bootprints of the Marine ahead of him, trying to avoid stepping out of line and onto an explosive.

Ridgeway had made it through a canal, but a Marine several meters behind him had stepped on an IED, causing an explosion that shattered all of the bones in one of his legs. Ridgeway administered basic first aid on the Marine, cleared a landing zone for a medevac helicopter, and found five bombs that had been buried in the surrounding area, which he disarmed.

Despite having such an action-packed morning, Ridgeway opted to go on another patrol later that same day. Soon after beginning the patrol, a lance corporal stepped on a bomb. Three of his limbs were blown off right away. Ridgeway then took control, ordering the other men not to move, while he crawled to the wounded man and even disarmed a bomb sitting in his path.

Ridgeway cleared an area for the helicopter while a corpsman treated the wounded soldier. By the end of the day, Ridgeway had disarmed at least eight bombs. He was awarded the Silver Star for assisting the wounded soldiers and for saving the lives of numerous other soldiers by disarming the bombs.

Corporal Jonathan Ayers

SILVER STAR RECIPIENT

Jonathan Ayers was from Snellville, Georgia. From a young age, his family knew that the military would be in Jonathan's future. He enlisted in the Army in April of 2006.

Ayers was deployed to Afghanistan as part of Operation Enduring Freedom, and he had one week remaining in his tour in 2008. His parents were planning a homecoming party for his arrival in three weeks.

▼ *Jonathan Ayers (middle) positioning a machine gun in Afghanistan*

▲ *Josh Ayers, Jonathan's brother, displays Jonathan's Silver Star.*

However, on July 13, 2008, Ayers was killed, along with eight other soldiers, on one of the worst dates for casualties during the War on Terror. While located the Combat Outpost Kahler, a newly-established base in Afghanistan near the Pakistan border, around 200 Taliban fighters attacked the small base where Ayers was stationed. It was estimated that there were at least twice as many Taliban insurgents as Coalition Forces during the attack.

According to witnesses that day, Ayers used his machine gun to keep the enemy forces away. He did not even cease firing when a bullet grazed his head. He only stopped once he was shot and killed by enemy fire. It is estimated that more than 100 of the 200 enemy fighters were killed or wounded during the battle. However, nine U.S. soldiers were killed, and 15 were wounded.

Ayers was posthumously awarded the Silver Star for his actions that day. The award was presented to his parents, Bill and Suzanne. Jonathan was remembered for being a good and caring man. He was 24 years old when he died.

Warrant Officer John W. Hermann

SILVER STAR RECIPIENT

John W. Hermann was from Tucson, Arizona, and deployed to Helmand Province in Afghanistan twice. During his first tour in 2008, Hermann was a staff sergeant and working as a bomb technician near a village called Dahaneh.

On February 26, 2008, his squad was attacked by enemy fighters armed with mortars, grenades, small arms, and machine-guns. Herman and another Marine charged toward the enemy. Herman proceeded to kill insurgents, and he braved machine gun fire to find and help a wounded Marine. He administered medical care to the wounded man and then returned to fighting position, despite shrapnel wounds in his legs. He proceeded to kill even more enemy fighters.

Hermann's actions not only saved the wounded Marine, but allowed the rest of the troops to safely clear the village. He was awarded the Silver Star for his actions.

▼ *John Hermann (right) is congratulated for his Silver Star.*

Army Specialist Ricardo Cerros

SILVER STAR RECIPIENT

▲ *Ricardo Cerros, Sr. and Marguerite Quiroz, Ricardo Cerros' parents, accept the Silver Star Medal on behalf of their fallen son.*

Ricardo Cerros was from Salina, California, and enlisted in the Army in July 2010, after graduating from the University of California, Irvine. He was 24 years old when he was deployed to Afghanistan, where he was known as a talented and well-respected member of his battalion.

On October 7, 2011, Cerros was on a mission on Logar province in Afghanistan. His team came under an enemy attack while patrolling an alleyway. One man was injured by gunfire, and as a medic came to aid him, a grenade was thrown into the alley. Spotting the danger, Cerros threw himself on top of the grenade, using his body to shield the blow from his men. He saved the lives of the men he was with, but Cerros himself was killed.

Cerros was posthumously awarded the Silver Star Medal for his bravery that day and for sacrificing his own life to save the lives of his fellow soldiers. His parents accepted the medal on his behalf.

Petty Officer First Class Benny Flores

SILVER STAR RECIPIENT

Hospital Corpsman First Class Benny Flores was deployed to southwestern Afghanistan as part of Operation Enduring Freedom. He had previously deployed to Iraq and Kuwait. While in Afghanistan, Flores served as the field service medical technician for the Marines stationed in Nimruz Province.

On April 28, 2012, two months into his tour, Flores and his convoy were attacked by a suicide bomber while driving in a convoy of unarmored pickup trucks. Flores was injured in the bombing. He was badly burned and bleeding from shrapnel wounds. However, disregarding his own injuries, he knew that he needed to check on his fellow Marines for serious injuries. One Marine, Sgt. Scott Pruitt, was fatally injured in the bombing, with deep shrapnel wounds to his neck and legs. Flores administered medical aid on Pruitt anyway, praying that he could be saved.

The attack was not over with the suicide bomber, however, and the enemy continued to ambush them with small-arms fire. Flores risked his life by running through the gunfire in order to save his fellow Marines and the Afghan police officer who had been working with them. He ran back and forth four times to assist the wounded men.

▶ *Flores is presented a Silver Star.*

Flores had to be hospitalized for the injuries he sustained that day. In addition to his wounds, he suffered a concussion. He did not think about his own injuries until every Marine was brought to the helicopter and taken to safety.

Flores was awarded the Silver Star for his actions, as well as a Purple Heart.

▼ *Benny Flores after receiving a Purple Heart*

Sergeant First Class Alicia Hofmann

SOLDIER'S MEDAL RECIPIENT

▲ *Hofmann is awarded the Soldier's Medal by Brig. Gen. Aaron Walter.*

Sgt. First Class Alicia Hofmann was from Cuyahoga Falls, Ohio, and served as an Army Reserve medic in Afghanistan, as well as a civilian registered nurse.

On October 4, 2014, Hofmann was driving down the interstate in Saline, Michigan, when she noticed a car that had hit a guardrail was on fire. She pulled over, called 911, and ran toward the burning vehicle. Hofmann saw that the man who had been driving was losing consciousness, and she tried to pull him out. However, he weighed an estimated 300 pounds, and Hofmann could not save him by herself.

She flagged down another car, driven by an Army National Guard Soldier, Spc. Bryant Williams. Hoffman reassured Williams to not be nervous and to use the skills he had learned in Army training. Together, Hofmann and Williams pulled the man out of the car. Police officers and firefighters arrived shortly after.

On September 29, 2017, Hofmann was awarded the Soldier's Medal for saving the man's life. She credits her Army training with giving her the skills needed to act heroically in a time of dire need.

Staff Sergeant Tyrone Mitchell

SOLDIER'S MEDAL RECIPIENT

▲ *Staff Sgt. Tyrone Mitchell (right) receives the Soldier's Medal.*

In May 2012, Staff Sgt. Tyrone A. Mitchell was driving down a road in Spring Lake, North Carolina, when he noticed an overturned vehicle on the side of the road. The vehicle had hit a fence and a concrete pillar before flipping over. Mitchell approached the vehicle and saw that the driver was conscious. However, he soon noticed a haze in the car, and realized that a part of the car may have set fire. Unable to open the driver's side door because it was locked, Mitchell retrieved a knife and broke a window with the knife's butt. Entering the vehicle, he pulled the driver from her seat and brought her to safety.

Emergency personnel arrived and evaluated Mitchell and the passenger of the car. The woman had injuries to both knees, and Mitchell had deep cuts in his arms, fingers, and wrist, but both were ultimately okay.

Mitchell was awarded the Soldier's Medal by his unit for his actions saving the woman from her car.

Specialist Nathan Currie

SOLDIER'S MEDAL RECIPIENT

On a calm morning in Georgia in August of 2014, Army Spc. Nathan Currie was out fishing when he heard a splashing sound suddenly come from the water. Looking toward the direction from where the sound had come, he initially thought it was just somebody's boat parked in the water. However, it finally dawned on him that it was a car, and it was floating away.

The woman who had been driving the car, Lora Chancey, had been driving along the nearby road when she swerved to avoid hitting a group of deer running by. The next thing she knew, she and her car were both floating in the muddy, alligator-infested water.

Currie ran to his car and called 911 before heading toward the water. Jumping in, he tried to keep his head above the brown, slimy water while feeling around inside the car for a body. He eventually realized that he'd have to go under, and swam into the car. Once inside, he found Chancey, who had been under water for about five minutes by the time he got to her.

▶ *Spc. Nathan Currie hugs Lora Chancey after receiving the Soldier's Medal.*

Currie proceeded to perform CPR on Chancey, losing hope with every breath. Finally, he heard her cough. She had survived the drowning.

Currie and his wife visited Chancey in the hospital during the following days. Chancey credits Currie with saving her life and being a hero.

Currie was awarded the Soldier's Medal in 2015 for his lifesaving actions.

► *Nathan Currie*

▼ *Brig. Gen. James Blackburn presents Nathan Currie with the Soldier's Medal.*

Staff Sergeant Robert Proffitt
MILITARY HERO

Air Force Staff Sgt. Robert Proffitt was enjoying a summer day at the beach in South Carolina in August 2012. He was wading in the water when he began to hear the faint sounds of screams coming from the ocean. A 7-year-old girl had gotten stuck in the riptide and was getting pulled into the ocean.

Proffitt swam towards the girl, who had sunken almost completely under the water by the time he got to her. While quickly running out of energy, Proffitt carried the girl on his back as he slowly swam more than 100 yards back to the beach. Once back on land, he called for help. The girl survived and was safely taken back to her parents.

Saving that girl from drowning was not the first time Proffitt saved a life. Several months before that incident, another Staff Sergeant at Proffitt's job began choking on a turkey sandwich during lunch. Proffitt performed the Heimlich maneuver on his friend until the piece of turkey shot across the room.

Proffitt credits his Air Force training with his ability to think and act quickly under pressure, and does not believe that he is a hero.

▶ *A photo of Staff Sgt. Robert Proffitt*

▼ *The beach at Sullivan's Island, South Carolina, where the young girl almost drowned*

Staff Sergeant Joseph Riemer

MILITARY HERO

▲ *A photo of Joseph Riemer while stationed in Alaska*

Staff Sgt. Joseph Riemer was deployed to Papua New Guinea as an explosive ordinance disposal technician in 2014.

While sitting at a hotel one night, he suddenly heard screams coming from outside. Riemer ran outside and found a local man drenched in blood. The man had been stabbed three times, and although Riemer was discouraged from helping due to the AIDS epidemic in Papua New Guinea, he proceeded to administer medical assistance to the man. He applied pressure to the wounds to help stop blood loss, but Riemer admits that he thought the man was going to die. He continued applying pressure to the wounds as he ordered someone to call an ambulance. The bleeding gradually lessened, but the ambulance never came. Riemer made sure the man got to the hospital by hotel transportation, and he was later informed that the man survived. If not for Riemer, the man likely would have died.

Riemer was nominated for the Noncommisioned Officers Association Vanguard Award because of his brave actions that day. The award recognizes enlisted members who perform heroic acts while off duty.

Private Terrance Bob
MILITARY HERO

On December 8, 2011, Pvt. Terrance Bob was at the DMV in Clarksville, Tennessee. He was there to take a driver's license test. He suddenly heard the sound of children screaming, and a woman behind him pointed out a minivan across the street that had caught on fire.

Bob threw his study papers on the ground and ran over to the burning van, nearly getting hit by a truck while running across the street. Getting closer and closer to the van, he realized that it had three children inside, all under the age of 10. Bob pulled all three of them out of the car, talking to them and keeping them calm until the police arrived.

Bob was nominated for an award for his actions that day. His commander, Staff Sgt. Lovie Moore hopes that Bob's actions provide a good example of what the Army stands for—putting others before oneself.

▼ *Pvt. Terrance Bob is applauded for heroically saving three children from a burning vehicle.*

Sergeant Michael Joseph
MILITARY HERO

▲ *Sgt. Michael Joseph (right) receives the Emergency Cardiovascular Care Heart Saver Award.*

On February 17, 2015, Sgt. Michael Joseph was leaving a training session at a movie theater on the Marine Corps Base in Hawaii. While he was walking out of the theater, Joseph heard a thud and a car alarm go off, and he saw a Marine fall to the ground and stop moving and breathing.

Joseph called emergency services and performed CPR on the fallen Marine until paramedics arrived.

Joseph had known what to do because his own brother passed away due to cardiac arrest when he was only 18 years old. After that, Joseph made sure to get CPR certified.

Joseph received the Emergency Cardiovascular Care Heart Save Hero Award from the American Heart Association because of his actions in saving the Marine's life. Joseph remained humble upon being called a hero, stating that he was just doing what anyone else would have done in the same situation.

Tech Sergeant Shaun Russell and Staff Sergeant Joseph Stalzer

MILITARY HEROES

▲ *Tech Sgt. Shaun Russell (left) and Staff Sgt. Joe Stalzer (right) stand with Denisse Willis.*

In January 2016 in Great Falls, Montana, a woman named Denisse Willis was in her car with her 18-month-old daughter, Aryanna, when Aryanna began having a seizure triggered by a fever. Willis pulled over to the side of the road, yelling at someone in a car behind her to call 911.

Meanwhile, Tech Sgt. Shaun Russell and two other airmen were passing by when they noticed the vehicle on the side of the road and Willis and her baby standing outside of it. They pulled over and checked Aryanna's vitals, rolling her on her side to open her airway.

Then, Staff Sgt. Joseph Stalzer arrived and performed a jaw thrust maneuver on Aryanna to open her airway. The men gave the baby their jackets to keep her warm. Emergency personnel arrived, taking Aryanna to the hospital for additional care.

Sergeant Mark Andrisek, Sergeant Joshua Sears, and Specialist Garrett "Doc" Young

MILITARY HEROES

Sgt. Mark Andrisek, Sgt. Joshua Sears, and Spc. Garrett "Doc" Young arrived in Afghanistan in July 2017. In November 2017, the men were stationed in Kandahar Province when they encountered an Afghan suicide vehicle. These suicide bombings were a common occurrence for their platoon in Afghanistan, and this was not the first time they encountered one.

During this incident, the bomb's blast caused a U.S. vehicle to spin off the road and flip over into a ravine. The driver and passenger of the vehicle were seriously injured. Spc. Garret "Doc" Young administered emergency medical aid to the driver's burns. Upon learning that there was a second soldier inside the vehicle, Sgt. Sears climbed in, despite the fact that the vehicle was on fire.

Sgt. Mark Andrisek began trying to put out the fires while sweeping for more explosive devices in the area so that a helicopter could make an emergency landing. Medivac helicopters were able to land and take away the wounded.

The three men received Army Commendation Medals for their bravery, but they say that their biggest reward is that no one died that day.

◄ *(Top left) Andrisek, Sears, and Young are honored for their actions.*

◄ *(Bottom left) Sgt. Mark Andrisek is pinned with the Army Commendation Medal.*

Corporal Joe L. Wrightsman

MILITARY HERO

Joe L. Wrightsman was born in 1987 and grew up in Kitsap County, Washington. He moved to Jonesboro, Louisiana, when he was thirteen. At Jonesboro Hodge High School, Wrightman excelled in sports and was known as a leader among fellow students.

Wrightsman had always aspired to join the Marines, and he enlisted in May 2005. He deployed twice to Iraq, and a third time to Afghanistan, despite his family's protests that he should not volunteer to go to Afghanistan. He went anyway, serving in counterinsurgency operations in partnership with Afghan National Security Forces.

▼ *Sgt. Joe L. Wrightsman's memorial service in Afghanistan, about two weeks after his death*

▲ *Marines from Wrightsman's squad in Afghanistan embrace one another after a memorial service for their fallen brother.*

▶ *A photo of Wrightsman at a memorial service*

In July 2010, Wrightman was wading through Helmand River with his unit and a group of Afghan trainees. He successfully made it across the river, but turned around to notice that his Afghan partner was having a hard time in the water. The man was getting swept away in the river.

Wrightsman dove into the water to rescue his partner, despite not knowing how to swim. His fellow Marines tried to rescue him, but they were unsuccessful. After two days of searching by the Marine Expeditionary Force, both Wrightman's body and the body of the Afghan soldier were recovered about a mile away from where they went missing.

Wrightsman is buried at Arlington National Cemetery.

Sergeant Kevin Peach

MILITARY HERO

In 2015, Sgt. Kevin Peach was driving down I-5 in California on his way to Marine Corps Base Camp when he saw a car on the highway swerve, hit a wall, and roll over. Peach pulled over to assist the man who had been driving the car.

Peach noticed smoke in the vehicle and realized that the car would likely catch fire. After unsuccessfully trying to break in the car's windows, a friend of Peach's broke the back windshield, and Peach went inside to search for bodies. He found a man who had been tangled up in seatbelts, but Peach could not get him free.

Peach had to cut the man out of the tangled seatbelt and carry him out. He attended to the man's injuries until an ambulance arrived. Peach had to be hospitalized for smoke inhalation.

In August 2017, Peach was awarded a Navy and Marine Corps Medal for his actions.

◀ *(Top left) Kevin Peach is awarded the Navy and Marine Corps Medal.*

◀ *(Bottom left) Sgt. Kevin Peach at the ceremony for his medal*

Major William Chesarek
MILITARY HERO

After attending flight school in both Pensacola, Florida, and Corpus Christi, Texas, Marine Corps Major William Chesarek, Jr. joined the RAF squadron in 2005, and by 2006 he was working in radio communication while deployed to Basra, Iraq.

On the night of June 10, while listening to the radio, he overheard that a group of insurgents was attacking British ground troops. In an attempt to distract the insurgents, Chesarek decided to fly low over the fighters, making himself their new target. He narrowly avoided being hit with a grenade, but continued to assist as much as he could. Upon hearing that there was an injured British soldier on the ground, Chesarek landed his helicopter, and a crew member jumped out to rescue the man.

Because of his actions in rescuing the British soldier, Chesarek was awarded the British Distinguished Flying Cross by Queen Elizabeth II. He was the first U.S. serviceman to receive this award since World War II.

▶ *William Chesarek with his Distinguished Flying Cross Award*

Captain Brian Jordan

MILITARY HERO

Brian Jordan was raised in Corpus Christi, Texas, in a military family. His dad was a Navy flight instructor, and this instilled a love of flying in young Brian. He completed Marine Corps Officer Candidate School between his junior and senior years of college.

In 2012, Jordan deployed to Afghanistan. Part of his duties in Afghanistan included providing cover for the British Grenadier Guards located in Helmand Province. However, the enemy was able to pin down the British soldiers during an attack, and Jordan and his crew witnessed an explosion shortly after. It turned out that one of the guardsmen had stepped on an explosive device, triggering an explosion that caused him to lose a limb.

Since emergency medical services would not be able to arrive for at least a half hour, Jordan and his crew decided to rescue the wounded British men themselves. This required putting themselves in harms way and exposing themselves to the enemy fighters. They pulled the wounded soldiers onto their aircraft and headed to get medical attention for their wounds. Both of the men survived.

► *Capt. Brian Jordan*

▲ *The British Distinguished Flying Cross*

Because of his role in rescuing the two British guardsmen, Brian Jordan was honored with the British Distinguished Flying Cross. He is the second American Marine since World War II to receive the award. The award is meant for aviators who show "exemplary gallantry in the air in presence of the enemy," and it is the equivalent of the United States' Silver Star.

Jordan denies being a hero, saying that he was merely doing his job. He gives credit to the flight crew that assisted him in rescuing the men.

Captain Barry F. Crawford
MILITARY HERO

▲ *Capt. Barry Crawford receiving the Air Force Cross*

On May 4, 2010, Capt. Barry F. Crawford was stationed in Afghanistan, serving as the Joint Terminal Attack Controller for a commando team. Crawford was leading a helicopter assault during a mission to collect intelligence on the Taliban from a remote village. Upon landing, the team soon realized that the village had been abandoned. The enemy fighters discovered their location and began an assault. The enemy force was made up of more than 100 fighters who had been hiding in the mountainside. They were using machine guns as well as snipers to attack Crawford and his crew. Fire rained down on them for more than ten hours.

Two Afghan soldiers in Crawford's team were killed, and three were severely wounded in the attack. Crawford exposed himself to enemy fire so that a helicopter could locate the injured men and get close enough to land and evacuate them. Crawford proceeded to fire back at the enemy, engaging in an attack. He also stood in the way of fire while he directed more than 33 aircraft toward the enemy force.

Crawford's men were ambushed several more times and began running out of ammunition. Crawford was able to coordinate an air attack of bombs that allowed his men to safely evacuate the village. More than 80 insurgents were killed during the battle.

Crawford received the Air Force Cross for his selfless actions that day. If he had not acted the way he did, many more lives could have been lost. He is only the fifth recipient of the award since September 11, 2001.

◀ *Crawford in Afghanistan*

▼ *Crawford during a press briefing at the Pentagon*

Officer Terrell Horne III

MILITARY HERO

Petty Officer Terrell Edwin Horne III was born in California in 1978 and enlisted in the U.S. Coast Guard in 1999. Horne served in the Coast Guard for almost 14 years and earned two Coast Guard Achievement Medals during his time of service.

In December 2012, 34-year-old Horne was investigating a vessel off the California Coast. The vessel was suspected to be the site of a drug smuggling operation. Horne was stationed aboard Coast Guard Cutter *Halibut* in Marina Del Rey.

While they were approaching the suspicious vessel, it suddenly sped directly toward *Halibut* and struck it. Horne pushed one of his crewmen out of the way of danger, but was propelled overboard while doing so. Horne was injured, but made it back to the boat safely. However, he sustained a serious head injury and was pronounced dead when the *Halibut* returned to port.

► *The dedication ceremony for a building in California renamed the Terrell E. Horne III Building*

▼ *The USCGC* Halibut

▲ *Coast Guard officers conduct a volley at a memorial service for Horne.*

▶ *Terrel Horne III during water survival training*

The suspects on the smuggling vessel were later detained and sentenced to life in prison for killing an officer, an extremely serious offense.

Horne was posthumously promoted to senior chief petty officer for his actions and for most likely saving the life of the crewman who he pushed out of the way. It was also announced that a Sentinel class cutter would be named after Horne. Additionally, the Coast Guard named its Terminal Island building after Horne.

Horne had two sons, and his wife was pregnant with another child at the time of the incident. She gave birth to another son only ten weeks after her husband's death.

Corporal Kyle Cameron

MILITARY HERO

Lance Cpl. Kyle C. Cameron was from Yakima, Washington. He graduated from East Valley High School in Yakima, and then went on to serve in the U.S. Military. He has stated that the best part about being deployed is the camaraderie shared between Marines.

When he was 20 years old, Cameron was deployed to Afghanistan. While stationed there, his squad was attacked by enemy fighters. Cameron safely made it to a covered position, but noticed a young Afghan boy who had been injured by enemy fire. Cameron braved the dangerous gunfire to rescue the boy and carry him to safety. However, he was ultimately unable to save the boy's life.

Cameron's actions earned him the Navy and Marine Corps Achievement Medal.

▲ *Cpl. Kyle Cameron*

▶ *The Navy and Marine Corps Achievement Medal*

Jeffrey Michael Ross

CITIZEN HONORS RECIPIENT

On July 12, 2009, former-Marine Jeffrey Michael Ross was driving to work when he noticed a commotion at the side of the road near a canal. He pulled over and realized that a black SUV had driven off the road, through a fence, and into the canal. Since no one else seemed to be helping, Ross dove into the water to save the woman trapped inside the car.

Ross swam over to the car and was able to reach through a small gap in its window. He then used the control button to roll down the rest of the window, causing the car to quickly fill with water. Acting fast, Ross tugged at the seatbelt of the woman in the vehicle, attempting to loosen it. Two more men eventually swam out to help. The three men loosened the seatbelt enough to free the woman, but just as they did, the car went completely underwater with the woman still inside. Luckily, she soon floated to the water's surface and was brought safely to land, where police officers and firefighters were waiting to assist her. She ultimately survived the incident.

Ross was nominated for the Citizen Service Above Self award for his actions that day. The award recognizes three people every year who commit acts of courage and self-sacrifice.

▼ *Jeffrey Michael Ross is awarded the Citizen Service Above Self medal.*

Dylan Nelson

CITIZEN HONORS RECIPIENT

▲ *Dylan Nelson's parents accept the Citizen Service Above Self medal on their son's behalf.*

Dylan Nelson was born in 1990 in Sioux Falls, South Dakota. When he was 18 years old, Nelson became a member of the 115th Network Support Company in the South Dakota National Guard. He was known as a sweet, selfless person with a heart of gold.

In 2009, Nelson was swimming in Lake Madison in South Dakota with his younger brother and his cousin. Suddenly, a strong current pulled the three young men underwater. Nelson escaped the current, but he went back into it to save his 14-year-old cousin and 15-year-old brother, who were still stuck in the water. Dylan was able to save them, but he disappeared in the process.

Dylan's body was not recovered until 10:30 that night.

Nelson's parents accepted many awards on their son's behalf. First, they accepted a Soldier's Medal. Then, in 2010, they accepted the Citizen Service Above Self medal.

▲ *Marine Cpl. Christopher Conley receives the Citizen Service Before Self medal on behalf of his mother, Marie Conley.*

In 2008, Marie Conley was a crossing guard in Boston. While trying to shield a young boy from a speeding car one day, Conley was struck by the car. She was taken to the hospital in critical condition, and she remained there in an induced coma.

Her son, Marine Cpl. Christopher Conley, was stationed in Iraq at the time, but he was pulled out of a mission so he could be with his mother during her last days. While he was devastated by the news of his mother, Cpl. Conley stated that he was not surprised to hear that she sacrificed her life to save a child.

Because of her heroic actions, Marie Conley was selected among hundreds of applicants to posthumously receive the Citizen Service Before Self honor. Her son accepted the honor on her behalf.

Dr. Jordy Cox
CITIZEN HONORS RECIPIENT

Jordy Cox, a trauma surgeon from Phoenix, Arizona, is known for traveling all over the world to volunteer his time and talents to perform life-saving surgeries on people who may not normally receive proper medical attention.

In 2008, Cox traveled to the Congo, despite the threat of civil war and the sound of bombs detonating right outside his operating room. In 2010, he went on a trip to Haiti following the devastating earthquake in 2010. While there, he treated hundreds of residents who had been injured in the natural disaster. He stayed in Haiti for several weeks, despite the lack of a place to sleep and adequate medical resources. He ended up performing many surgeries in the middle of the streets.

In March 2010, Dr. Cox was awarded the Citizen Service Before Self medal for his selflessness and willingness to travel to faraway, potentially dangerous places in order to administer proper medical care to those in need.

▼ *Dr. Jordy Cox speaks at the ceremony at which he received the Citizen Service Before Self medal.*

Father Joe Carroll

CITIZEN HONORS RECIPIENT

Joe Carroll was born in the Bronx, New York, and he aspired to become a priest from an early age. After being ordained, he moved across the country to San Diego, California, where his efforts in helping the poor and homeless population have been widely praised and recognized on a national level.

In 1982, Father Joe became the president of a small food kitchen and thrift store dedicated to helping the homeless. He quickly expanded the organization, putting his efforts into fundraising and buying more property, so that it eventually spanned four blocks and provided not only meals, but housing, job counseling, and healthcare to the city's homeless population. Father Joe has raised millions of dollars for his organization.

In 2013, Father Joe was awarded the Citizen Service Before Self medal for his commitment to helping the homeless and the steps he is taking to alleviate the homelessness epidemic in the United States.

▼ *The Citizen Service Before Self medal is placed around Father Joe Carroll's neck.*

Jon Meis

CITIZEN HONORS RECIPIENT

▲ *Jon Meis (right) receives the Citizen Service Before Self medal from Medal of Honor recipient Patrick Brady.*

On a quiet morning in June 2014 at Seattle Pacific University, a gunman entered the school's campus and shot three students, one of whom died.

A 22-year-old electrical engineering student, Jon Meis, worked at a student security desk and was monitoring the hallways of the building when he heard the first shots ring out. Meis used pepper spray on the gunman while the man was trying to reload his gun. Meis then tackled him, taking the gun and hiding it in a separate room. This most likely prevented the shooter from injuring any more victims. Officers arrived and handcuffed the shooter. Meis was not harmed, but he was taken to the hospital anyway.

The shooter was identified as Aaron R. Ybarra, who was not a student at the university. Ybarra was taken to King County Jail and charged with premeditated first-degree murder and second-degree assault.

Meis had always been regarded as an exceptional student and friend, and he remained humble while the public praised him as a hero.

Alton Brieske

▲ *Alton Brieske receives the Citizen Service Before Self Medal from Medal of Honor recipient William Swenson.*

In 2014, 21-year-old Alton Brieske was a medical student at Florida Atlantic University. He was eating lunch one day when he heard a strange noise outside.

When he went to see what it was, he saw a car submerged in a nearby lake. Brieske and two other men jumped in the water and used a hammer to smash in the window of the car. The three of them rescued the unconscious 92-year-old man trapped in the car and dragged him to shore. The man was in critical condition, and Brieske, who dreamed of becoming an ER doctor some day, performed CPR on him until an ambulance came and the man was taken to the hospital. Officials were not sure what caused the man to drive into the lake.

Brieke refused to accept his title of "hero," claiming he had just been in the right place at the right time.

Petty Officer Third Class Rob Williams

DISASTER RELIEF

On September 1, 2005, Petty Officer 3rd Class Rob Williams of the U.S. Coast Guard was assisting in rescue efforts in New Orleans, Louisiana. A few days earlier, Hurricane Katrina had swept through New Orleans, causing the city's levee system to fail. New Orleans was completely flooded, and while some residents were able to escape before the levees broke, many were stuck stranded in the rising floodwaters.

More than 150 victims were stranded on the roof of a hotel, and it was up to Officer Williams to save them. When he disconnected

◄ *An aerial view of New Orleans and the flooding caused by Hurricane Katrina*

▼ *A military helicopter is loaded with supplies to bring to New Orleans.*

from the cable hoisting him down from a helicopter, three men approached him. They claimed to have a gun and that they would kill Williams if he did not assist them before assisting the others on the roof. Since they were not injured, they were not Williams' top priority, and he used his own knife to threaten them to back off.

Six victims on the roof were injured, and Williams helped them get into the helicopter to be treated and taken to safety. He then remained on the roof to comfort the other victims and assure them that they would all be taken to safety. He made sure that the violent men wielding weapons were taken away first in a helicopter, and then worked with four more helicopters to rescue the remaining 150 flood victims. Williams did not leave the roof until all of the victims had been evacuated.

During the entire course of the Hurricane Katrina relief efforts, Williams performed a total of 113 rescue missions.

Williams received the Coast Guard Medal for his bravery and direct assistance in saving hundreds of lives after Hurricane Katrina.

◄ *(Top left) Residents on the roof of a home flooded by Hurricane Katrina*

◄ *(Bottom left) Members of the Coast Guard approach a home in a flooded area while searching for survivors.*

Thad Allen
DISASTER RELIEF

Thad Allen was born in Tucson, Arizona, in 1949. His father was a U.S. Coast Guard damage controlman, so Allen grew up frequently moving from place to place. In 1971, Allen graduated from the United States Coast Guard Academy. He also has a master's degree from George Washington University and one from MIT.

After a long career overseeing operations all over the U.S. and the Caribbean, Allen went on to serve as the Coast Guard's Chief of Staff from 2002 until 2006.

After Hurricane Katrina struck New Orleans in 2005, Allen was put in charge of the recovery and relief efforts for the city after the removal of Michael D. Brown, the director of the Federal Emergency Management

▶ *Thad Allen, 2006*

▶ *President George W. Bush greets Lt. Gen. Russel Honore (middle) and Thad Allen (left) as they step onto a Naval Air Base in New Orleans in 2005.*

Agency. While leading these efforts, he was widely praised for his leadership and performance.

In 2010, Allen was named the National Incident Commander after the Deepwater Horizon oil spill in the Gulf of Mexico.

Allen retired from the Coast Guard in 2010, but he continued to serve as the Deepwater Horizon National Incident Commander for several months after his retirement.

Allen has received numerous awards for his leadership and service, including the Coast Guard Achievement Medal, the Humanitarian Service Medal, the Legion of Merit, and the Armed Forces Service Medal.

▲ *Allen briefs a command crew on the Deepwater Horizon oil spill.*

▶ *Allen (left) at a conference on Hurricane Awareness Day, May 28, 2008*

Captain Kevin Robinson and Captain Kevin Buckley

DISASTER RELIEF

In September of 2017, Puerto Rico was hit by the devastating Hurricane Maria, one of the worst natural disasters to ever occur in the region. Hundreds of people were killed in the storm's wake, and almost the entire island lost power, clean water, and cell phone service.

On September 29, the USNS *Comfort* set sail from Norfolk, Virginia, toward Puerto Rico, arriving in early October. The *Comfort* was a full-service hospital ship aiming to aid those who had been injured in the hurricane. Its mission commander was Captain Kevin Robinson. Over the course of 36 hours before its deployment, Robinson and his staff flew in hundreds of medical and support personnel from across the country to assist the *Comfort*'s mission.

The ship carried 800 medical personnel, who treated almost 2,000 patients and performed nearly 200 surgeries in their 53-day deployment.

▼ *The USNS* Comfort

Captain Kevin Buckley, the medical commanding officer on *Comfort*, said that bringing aid to Puerto Rico was the highlight of his career. Captain Robinson said that working on the *Comfort* changed his life. Both men are proud of the work their crew accomplished during their time in Puerto Rico, as well as the differences they made in so many people's lives.

◄ *(Top left) The governor of Puerto Rico visits the USNS* Comfort.

◄ *(Bottom left) Damage caused by Hurricane Maria*

▼ *Captain Kevin Robinson standing in front of the* Comfort

The Thai Cave Rescue
DISASTER RELIEF

On June 23, 2018, twelve boys from a soccer team, the Wild Boars, along with their coach, entered the Tham Laung caves in Thailand after their team practice. They intended a short visit. Instead, they were trapped by rising water from a rainstorm. On July 10, the last of the boys left the flooded caves, after a daring rescue that involved thousands of people, including more than 100 divers.

Although the disappearance of the boys and their coach was noted by the evening of the 23rd, divers were not able to reach the trapped boys until more than a week later, on July 2. During that time, the team drank water that dripped from the cave walls, played checkers, tried to dig, and meditated to stay calm. While they waited for rescue, a flurry of activity surrounded the caves. Volunteers from more than a dozen countries set out to offer technical know-how, rescue specialists, and equipment for diving and pumping water out of the caves. Millions of gallons of water had to be pumped out of the cave system before a rescue attempt could be made.

▼ *Inside the cave*

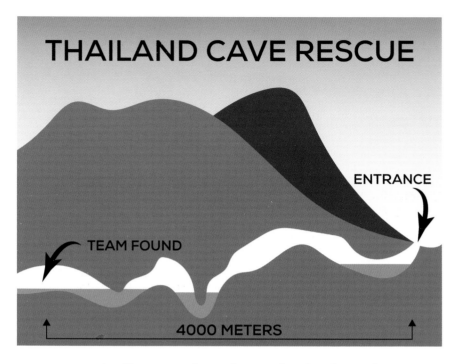

THAILAND CAVE RESCUE

ENTRANCE

TEAM FOUND

4000 METERS

▲ *An illustration shows the convoluted pathway the rescuers had to follow.*

▲ *Saman Kunan is honored with ceremonial offerings.*

▼ *The rescued boys hold a press conference on July 18.*

The technical challenges were immense. The monsoon season was beginning, the passages to reach the team were narrow, and the water was filled with silt that greatly reduced visibility—a threat even to experienced divers. Tragically, on July 6, one such diver died. Saman Kunan, a former Thai Navy SEAL, had placed air tanks along the route, but lost consciousness while making his way back to the cave entrance. He was posthumously promoted to lieutenant commander for his bravery and sacrifice.

After much planning, Thai Navy SEALs and experienced cave divers from several countries began to pull the team out of the cave on July 8. The boys were sedated so they would not panic while being carried underwater, and placed on flexible stretchers, with masks over their faces. Divers maneuvered the stretchers in teams. Over the course of three days, all the boys and their coach were rescued, emerging to the cheers of millions worldwide.

Jake Wood and William McNulty

DISASTER RELIEF

In January 2010, a magnitude 7.8 earthquake hit Haiti, affecting about three million people, killing more than 100,000 people, and causing hundreds of thousands of buildings to collapse.

While governments from around the world sent humanitarian aid to Haiti, two former Marines, Jake Wood and William McNulty, knew that they had to do their part to help. Having served in Iraq and Afghanistan with the Marines, Wood was used to helping people in dire need. They arrived in Haiti with an 8-person team of volunteers, all veterans of the U.S. military.

This was the start of Team Rubicon, the organization created by Wood and McNulty that has expanded to include more than 35,000 veteran volunteers. The organization focuses on helping populations that tend to be overlooked by other aid organizations.

> "The Marine Corps taught me many things, but one of the most important things it taught me was how to overcome seemingly impossible odds."
>
> —Jake Wood

▼ *Jake Wood in Haiti*

▼ *Port-au-Prince, Haiti, after the devastating earthquake in 2010*

Jorge Muñoz

PRESIDENTIAL CITIZENS MEDAL RECIPIENT

Jorge Muñoz was born in Palmira, Valle del Cauca, Colombia, in 1964, and moved to New York City with his mother when he was a teenager. Once in New York, he became a citizen of the United States and found a job as a bus driver.

In 2004, Muñoz began realizing how much food regularly went to waste throughout the city. He started a food collection from local businesses and restaurants and began handing out free meals to the city's homeless population. He was initially only able to provide free meals three nights a week, but eventually his family and friends joined him, and together they started serving meals daily. Muñoz contributed a large portion of his personal income to these efforts.

In 2006, Muñoz turned his efforts into a non-profit organization, the An Angel in Queens Foundation. Muñoz and his team serve meals every day of the year, and they have become an institution that New York's homeless population can rely on.

Muñoz was nominated as a Hero of the Year by CNN in 2009, and in 2010, he received the Presidential Citizens Medal from President Barack Obama. The Presidential Citizens Medal is the second highest award for civilian actions and service. The first is the Medal of Freedom.

Muñoz was also recognized by the Colombian government for his efforts in feeding homeless Latino immigrants in New York City.

▶ *Jorge Muñoz*

◀ *Palmira, Valle del Cauca, Colombia, Muñoz's birthplace*

Betty Chinn

PRESIDENTIAL CITIZENS MEDAL RECIPIENT

Betty Chinn grew up homeless in China. She eventually immigrated to the United States and now lives in Eureka, California, where she acts as an advocate for the city's homeless population. In 2013, Chinn assisted in opening a community center to aid in breaking the cycle of homelessness. Chinn's community center aims to help not only the homeless, but also the mentally ill, disabled veterans, and drug abusers.

The Betty Kwan Chinn Day Center provides case management, mental health services, job counseling, skill workshops, a computer lab, and a children's center. The center is run almost completely by volunteers, donations, and grants.

In 2017, after an electric company donated seven trailers to her organization, Chinn began a housing program to help homeless residents establish rental histories. The residents can pay a nominal rent fee to live in one of the trailers, therefore making them better candidates to rent from future landlords.

In 2010, Chinn was awarded the Presidential Citizens Medal by Barack Obama.

▲ *The Presidential Citizens Medal*

▲ *Betty Chinn*

Victoria Leigh Soto

PRESIDENTIAL CITIZENS MEDAL RECIPIENT

Victoria Soto was born in Bridgeport, Connecticut, in 1985 and graduated from Eastern Connecticut State University in 2008, enrolling in graduate school at Southern Connecticut University afterward. She went on to become a first grade teacher at Sandy Hook Elementary School.

On December 12, 2012, a gunman entered the elementary school, shooting at students and teachers. He entered Soto's classroom, where she attempted to hide her first grade students. As he tried to shoot at students, Soto threw herself in front of them, sacrificing her own life in order to save the first graders.

The gunman killed 20 students and 6 staff members in his rampage that day. It was one of the deadliest school shootings in U.S. history.

Soto was remembered in numerous different ways after her heroic death. The Victoria Leigh Soto Endowed Memorial Scholarship fund was created at Eastern Connecticut State University. The fund serves as a scholarship fund for students aspiring to become teachers. Several buildings were renamed after Soto in both the U.S. and in Puerto Rico, where her father was from.

Soto and the five other staff members killed in the Sandy Hook shooting were posthumously awarded the Presidential Citizens Medal by Barack Obama in 2013.

◀ *A memorial for those who died in the tragic Sandy Hook shooting*

Chanhpheng Sivila
HUMANITARIAN AND ACTIVIST

Chanhpheng Sivila grew up in Laos, and when she was only three years old, she contracted polio. Because the polio affected her ability to walk, her parents did not let her attend school with the rest of her 11 siblings. However, Chanhpheng stole her sister's uniform and secretly attended school one day. The schoolteachers eventually convinced her parents to let her attend.

In many developing countries, children with disabilities are often excluded from school and rarely receive an education because of widespread discriminatory attitudes toward those with disabilities. Chanhpheng, however, did not let her disability get in the way of her education. She eventually went on to earn a bachelor's degree from the National Academy of Politics and Public Administration in Vietnam and another degree in business administration from Rattana College in Laos.

In 1990, Chanhpheng founded the Lao Disabled Women's Development Center, and she currently works as an advocate for women and girls with disabilities. The center provides education, job training, and life skill training for 35 young women every year.

▼ *(Left) Chanhpheng Sivila holds up a scarf made by a young woman at the center.*

▼ *(Right) The United States Agency for International Development Senior International Education Advisor visits a class at the Lao Disabled Women's Development Center.*

Razia Jan

HUMANITARIAN AND ACTIVIST

▲ *Razia Jan in a community garden*

Born in Afghanistan in the 1940s, Razia Jan moved to the United States in 1970. Jan's philanthropic efforts started after September 11, 2001, when she and her community made blankets to send to the rescue workers at Ground Zero. She then began sending care packages to U.S. troops overseas, as well as over 30,000 pairs of shoes to children in need in Afghanistan.

In 2002, during a visit to Afghanistan, Jan saw firsthand how oppressed the women and girls were by the Taliban. Girls were often violently killed, just for trying to attend school. In 2005, Jan began a fundraising effort to build a school in Afghanistan. Her nonprofit is called Razia's Ray of Hope.

Through donations to the organization, Razia is able to provide completely free education for the girls who attend the school. The Zabuli Education Center offers math, science, religion, and language classes, and recently added a computer lab.

Jan was nominated for a CNN Hero of the Year Award in 2012.

Kakenya Ntaiya
HUMANITARIAN AND ACTIVIST

Kakenya Ntaiya was born in Kenya in 1978. She got engaged when she was only five years old, and underwent painful female genital mutilation in preparation for her marriage when she was a young teenager. However, Ntaiya aspired to a different life path than the one expected of her that demanded she become a wife and a mother. She enjoyed school and hoped to become a teacher, so she convinced her father to let her go to school. Ntaiya was eventually given a scholarship to a college in the United States. Upon leaving her village, she vowed to come back to help them.

In the United States, Ntaiya earned a bachelors degree, a doctorate in education, and a job at the United Nation. In 2008, she returned to

her village and opened a primary school for girls—the first school of its kind in the village. Eventually the school expanded to provide housing for its students so that they could spend more time focusing on their studies.

When parents enroll their daughters in the school, they must agree that they will not force their daughters to undergo female genital mutilation or early marriage.

In addition to the school, Ntaiya's nonprofit also started a series of leadership camps to teach young girls about public health issues, such as female circumcision, teen pregnancy, and HIV/AIDS. She hopes that through her nonprofits, girls will be inspired to follow their dreams.

Ntaiya has been nominated for and received numerous awards for her efforts, including being named a CNN Hero of the Year in 2013.

◄ *Kakenya Ntaiya (second from right)*

Nasrin Sotoudeh

HUMANITARIAN AND ACTIVIST

Nasrin Sotoudeh was born in Tehran, Iran, in 1963. She studied law at Shahid Beheshti University and went on to work in the legal department of the Iranian Ministry of Housing. In 1995, she passed the Bar exam and became a lawyer, focusing on human rights, particularly the defense of abused children and mothers. She became known for defending activists and journalists.

In 2010, Sotoudeh was arrested on the charges of spreading propaganda and conspiracy. While imprisoned, she was reportedly tortured and subjected to solitary confinement. In 2011, she was banned from practicing law, as well as from leaving the country for 20 years. This ban was eventually reduced.

In October of 2012, because of her firm defense of her beliefs and tendency to put others before herself, even in a situation as extreme as being imprisoned, Sotoudeh was awarded the Sakharov Prize. The prize honors those dedicated to human rights and freedom of thought.

▼ *A demonstration supporting Nasrin Sotoudeh in 2012*

Malala Yousafzai

HUMANITARIAN AND ACTIVIST

Malala Yousafzai was born in Mingora, Swat, Pakistan, in 1997. Her father, a poet and activist, encouraged her to become a politician, and the two would often spend nights discussing politics.

In the Swat Valley of northwest Pakistan, the Taliban were known to ban young girls from receiving education, listening to music, watching television, and going shopping. In 2008, when Yousafzai was only in the seventh grade, she began writing an anonymous blog detailing her life as a young woman living in Pakistan under Taliban rule.

As Yousafzai was writing the first of her blog posts, the Taliban were blowing up girls' schools. They then passed an edict banning girls from attending school after January 15, 2009. The schools were able to reopen by late February, under the condition that girls had to wear burqas, but the Taliban remained active in the area. The time of relative peace did not last long, and in May, Yousafzai and her family were displaced as the Pakistani Army entered the region in which they lived. They were able to return home in late July.

Eventually, Yousafzai's blogging identity was revealed and her public profile rose. She appeared on television to advocate for women's education, and she was the first Pakistani girl to be nominated for the International Children's Peace Prize. However, the public exposure meant Yousafzai's safety was compromised, and Taliban leaders unanimously decided to kill her in 2012.

In October of 2012, as 15-year-old Yousafzai was taking a bus home from school, she was confronted and shot by a Taliban gunman. She was airlifted to a military hospital, where doctors successfully

▶ *Malala Yousafzai at the* Glamour *Woman of the Year Awards in 2013*

removed the bullet lodged in her shoulder. She was transferred to several different hospitals, and came out of a coma in about a week.

Yousafzai's murder attempt was met with widespread outrage throughout the entire world. It also prompted the United Nations to release a petition demanding education for every child and the end to discrimination against women.

After her hospital release, Yousafzai continued advocating for education, and even confronted President Barack Obama for his use of drone strikes in Pakistan.

In 2014, Yousafzai was awarded the Nobel Peace Prize, becoming the youngest Nobel Laureate.

▼ *Yousafzai (third from left) at the Nobel Peace Prize ceremony, 2014*

Leymah Gbowee

HUMANITARIAN AND ACTIVIST

Leymah Gbowee was born in central Liberia in 1972. In 1989, when she was just 17 years old, the First Liberian Civil War began; it lasted until 1996. After the war, Gbowee enrolled in a training program run by UNICEF to become a counselor for those who had been traumatized during the war. During her training, Gbowee realized the she was in an abusive relationship herself, and she moved to Ghana in an attempt to find a more peaceful life for her family. While in Ghana, however, the family almost starved. They were virtually homeless and did not have a cent to their name. Gbowee and her children went back to Liberia.

In Liberia, Gbowee became an active volunteer at a Lutheran Church while working toward her degree in social work. The program in which she volunteered was called the Trauma Healing and Reconciliation Program.

After working there for a year, Gbowee was approached to help the West Africa Network for Peacebuilding begin a program dedicated to helping women. At the first meeting for the Women in Peacebuilding Network, Gbowee told the story of sleeping on the floor of the hospital after giving birth because she didn't have money to pay the hospital bills. She was then named the coordinator of Liberian Women's Initiatives.

▼ *Gbowee (back row, second from left) at the 2012 International Women of Courage Awards*

▲ *Gbowee at a Women for Peace parade in Jerusalem*

In 2002, while working in Liberia, Gbowee rallied a movement of women demanding peace. The movement included both Christian and Muslim women, and together they prayed for peace and held nonviolent protests calling for an end to the wars that had been devastating the country. The war officially ended weeks after Gbowee and the women protestors held demonstrations outside of hotels where peace talks were being negotiated.

The movement also assisted in the election of Ellen Johnson Sirleaf, the first woman president of Liberia.

After the end of the war, Gbowee went on to attend graduate school in the United States and win numerous awards and recognitions for her efforts in working toward women's equality and the end of poverty. As of 2017, she is the Executive Director of the Women, Peace, and Security Program at Columbia University.

Aki Ra

HUMANITARIAN AND ACTIVIST

Aki Ra was born in the 1970s in Cambodia and orphaned at a young age. He was raised to become a child soldier for the Khmer Rouge political regime, the same regime that killed his parents. When Cambodia was invaded by the Vietnamese army, Aki Ra was taken by Vietnamese soldiers and enlisted with the Kampuchean People's Revolutionary Armed Forces, where his duties included planting landmines along the border of Cambodia and Thailand.

In 1991, Aki Ra was hired by the UN as a deminer since he had so much experience laying landmines as a soldier. After his time with the UN, he began using simple tools like a knife, hoe, and stick to defuse unexploded landmines he found. Nearby people began seeking him out to defuse mines they found in their villages, and Aki Ra soon began an education program to teach people about unexploded mines. He collected the empty shells in his home, and soon started charging tourists a dollar to look at his collection, funding his activities with the profits. This marked the beginning of the Cambodian Landmine Museum.

While defusing mines in small villages, Aki Ra often encountered orphaned children, who he would bring home. Many had been affected by landmines, polio, or HIV. Aki Ra took in more than two dozen children, using funds from the museum to support them.

◄ *Aki Ra*

▲ *The entrance to the Cambodian Landmine Museum*

◄ *An example of a landmine*

In 2008, Aki Ra gained full certification as a deminer and established the Cambodian Self Help Demining, an NGO dedicated to clearing small villages of landmines. These villages are often overlooked by other organizations working in areas they deem to be higher priority.

Aki Ra has been awarded several peace awards and was named a CNN Hero in 2010. He has also been the subject of several books and a documentary.

Dr. Laura Stachel

HUMANITARIAN AND ACTIVIST

Dr. Laura Stachel is an obstetrician/gynecologist. She received a doctor of medicine degree at UC San Francisco and a master's of public health degree from UC Berkeley. In 2008, Stachel went to Nigeria to study maternal mortality rates. While there, she was shocked to see that the hospitals did not have adequate electricity, forcing doctors to conduct deliveries and caesarian sections in the dark or by flashlights. Sometimes they had to delay procedures until the next day, and the patients were forced to wait many hours to undergo life-saving procedures.

Stachel's husband was an energy educator, and together the pair designed a solar electric system for the hospital where Laura was studying. Employees at the hospital introduced Stachel to clinicians in nearby facilities, who asked for their own lighting systems. Soon, workers from around the world began requesting similar fixtures.

We Care Solar, the name of Stachel's organization, began manufacturing solar fixtures in 2011, and as of the end of 2016, around 1,900 solar fixtures had been sent to 27 different countries.

◄ *Dr. Laura Stachel after winning an award in Advacements for the Developing World*

Floyd Hammer and Kathy Hamilton

HUMANITARIANS AND ACTIVISTS

▲ *President Barack Obama awards Floyd Hammer and Kathy Hamilton the Daily Point of Light Award.*

In 2004, husband and wife Floyd Hammer and Kathy Hamilton were preparing to go on a cruise to celebrate their retirement, but decided at the suggestion of some friends to volunteer at an HIV/AIDS clinic in Tanzania instead.

Disturbed by the conditions they witnessed in Tanzania, including children who were dying from malnutrition, the couple decided to dedicate their time to fighting starvation. They founded a nonprofit called Outreach, which has distributed more than 229 million free meals to children since its beginning. The organization has expanded to send aid to more than 15 countries, including the United States, where child starvation is still a large issue.

In addition to providing free meals, Outreach also started conducting biannual medical missions, lasting eight-to-ten days each, as well as the construction of a farm and the installation of a system to sanitize water.

In July of 2013, Hammer and Hamilton received the Daily Point of Light Award, an award to celebrate Americans who selflessly make the world a better place.

Widad Akreyi

HUMANITARIAN AND ACTIVIST

Widad Akreyi was born in the Kurdistan Region of Iraq. Her passion for human rights started at a young age when she began working as an advocate for her school classmates.

She then went on to study civil engineering at Salahaddin University. In the late 1980s, she began secretly documenting human rights violations occurring in Iraq, collecting evidence of torture and other abuses by interviewing victims. In 1990, she began advocating for gender equality in the Middle East and co-founded a Women's Working Group to encourage women to participate in the call for peace. Akreyi was forced to leave Iraq in 1991.

Akreyi eventually earned a master's degree in genetics and genomics and a PhD in global health and cancer epidemiology. She has also continued working as an advocate for human rights, working for Amnesty International and as a co-chair of the Women's Working Group.

▲ *Widad Akreyi with the International Pfeffer Peace Prize*

▲ *Widad Akreyi at a memorial for Syrian refugees who passed away*

◄ *Widad Akreyi*

In addition to working toward eradicating torture and gender-based violence, Akreyi has spoken out expressing concern for displaced populations and refugees, particularly the more than 2,500 Syrian refugees who died while escaping to Europe in 2015. She also works to end executions of child domestic workers, and she campaigns to end human trafficking.

Akreyi has won numerous awards for her activism, including the Fellowship of Reconciliation award and the International Pfeffer Peace Award.

Runcie C. W. Chidebe

HUMANITARIAN AND ACTIVIST

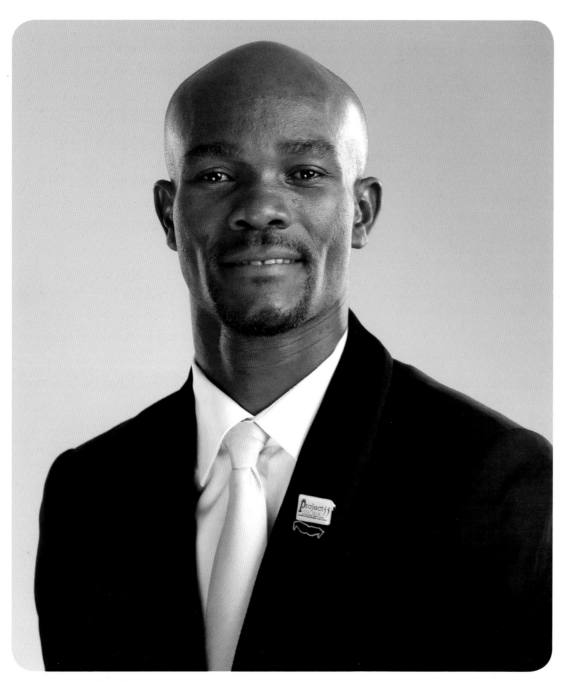

Runcie Chidebe was born in Nigeria in 1985. He holds a diploma in social work as well as a bachelor's degree in psychology/sociology and anthropology.

In 2013, Chidebe founded Project Pink Blue and Health & Psychological Trust Centre. The organization focuses on spreading awareness of cancer. They provide free cancer screenings and support resources for people with cancer in rural or impoverished communities. Project Pink Blue focuses particularly on breast cancer, and has provided more than 700 women with free screenings.

Chidebe has also called for Nigeria's government to establish a National Agency on Cancer Control. He has won numerous humanitarian awards for his work and was named one of the top 1000 African entrepreneurs in 2015.

◄ *Runcie Chidebe*

Nadia Sharmeen

HUMANITARIAN AND ACTIVIST

Nadia Sharmeen is a crime journalist from Bangladesh. She aspired to become a journalist from a young age, and she started her career as a crime reporter in 2009.

In 2013, while covering an Islamic rally demanding stronger restrictions on women, as well as harsher punishment of atheists, Sharmeen was brutally attacked. The group who attacked her, the Hefazat-e-Islam activists, often targeted journalists. At the rally, they were specifically targeting women who were not wearing the hijab.

Between 50 and 60 men chased Sharmeen, throwing water bottles and bricks at her. They then punched her and beat her. Sharmeen was taken to the hospital and stabilized. However, no arrests came out of the attack, despite the fact that many photos were taken of the assaulters and they could be easily identified.

After the attack, Sharmeen returned to crime reporting. She became a model for women's rights activists. In 2014, Sharmeen was honored with the International Women of Courage Award by the U.S. State Department.

◄ *(Top left) Sharmeen at the International Women of Courage Awards*

◄ *(Bottom left) Sharmeen (far left) with the other recipients of the IWCA and First Lady Michelle Obama*

Niloofar Rahmani

HUMANITARIAN AND ACTIVIST

Born in Kabul, Afghanistan in 1992, Niloofar Rahmani was inspired by female helicopter pilots of the Soviet era, and she dreamed of becoming a pilot from an early age. She spent a year studying English so she would be able to attend flight school, and in 2012 she graduated from the Afghan Air Force Officer Training Program as a Second Lieutenant.

After attending advanced flight school, Rahmani began flying a military cargo aircraft. During one mission, when she discovered injured soldiers, she flew them to the hospital. Since women were normally banned from transporting dead or wounded soldiers, when Rahmani's achievements were publicized, she and her family began receiving threats from the Taliban. Her family was forced to move, but this did not stop Rahmani from attending more pilot training programs, including programs in the United States Air Force.

Rahmani was awarded the International Women of Courage Award in 2015 for standing up for women's rights in the face of hateful threats.

◄ *(Top left) Rahmani accepting her pilot wings in 2013*

◄ *(Bottom left) Niloofar Rahmani with female pilots from the U.S. Marine Corps*

▲ *Gandhi unveiling a plaque at St. Michael's School*

▲ *Gandhi after receiving the Children's Hope India Award*

Meera Gandhi was born in Mumbai, India, in 1963. She received a bachelor's degree in economics from the University of Delhi, and an M.B.A. from the Boston University School of Management. She also attended the Executive Education Program at Harvard Business School.

In 2010, Gandhi started the Giving Back Foundation. The foundation aims to aid those suffering from illness and poverty, with a particular interest in women and children's issues.

One of her main projects is New Delhi's St. Michael's School in India. Gandhi's foundation ensures that the students at the school receive daily meals and updated classrooms and school grounds.

Gandhi's foundation also awards many scholarships and grants to different students and charities, particularly ones with strong female leadership.

Gandhi is the recipient of numerous awards for her services, including the Ellis Island Medal of Honor, Corporate Global Humanitarian award, and Children's Hope Humanitarian award.

MAESTRO CARES
FOUNDATION